Robert Rushm

Sage House

Fanny Kemble

A crayon portrait of Fanny Kemble by Sir Thomas Lawrence

by ROBERT RUSHMORE

Crowell-Collier Press
Collier-Macmillan Limited, London

for
Catharine S. Huntington
whom
Fanny Kemble
would have admired

Library of Congress Catalog Card Number: 70-95176

The Macmillan Company
Collier-Macmillan Canada Ltd., Toronto, Ontario

Printed in the United States of America

FIRST PRINTING

Portrait of Fanny Kemble reproduced with the permission of The Metropolitan Museum of Art, Gift of George D. Pratt, 1935

Contents

PART ONE

PART TWO

Contents

Acknowledgments

I am grateful to the New York Society Library for providing certain material invaluable to the writing of this book. My wife has painstakingly proofread it and provided the index.

Part One

The death I should prefer would be
to break my neck off the back of a good
horse at a full gallop on a fine day.

—Fanny Kemble

CHAPTER 1

The Covent Garden Theatre

EARLY ON THE morning of September 20, 1808, fire broke out in London's famous Covent Garden Theatre located in the wholesale produce section of Europe's greatest city. A new water main was being installed in the teeming quarter, and when the fire engines rushed on to the scene for over an hour they had no water with which to fight the tremendous blaze. After that it was too late. Brave men, loving the fine old building and not thinking of their lives, moved an engine into a section of the theater and moments later the roof collapsed upon them. Twenty died in all; others, burned so terribly that their relatives scarcely recognized them, were taken to nearby hospitals. In three hours everything was gone, a vast collection of scenery, costumes, and stage properties as well as a fine library of plays and books on dramas. The great composer George Frederick Handel had donated an organ to the theater to be used when oratorios were performed. This too was destroyed together with a number of the composer's original scores—irreplaceable, having been written in his own hand.

Worst of all was the loss of the actual theater itself, lying now in desolate ashes—the theater that for so many years had been connected with the remarkable family of actors called Kemble.

Of the twelve children born to Roger Kemble, an actor of Irish descent well known in England, eight survived. Of these, at least five had played at the famous theater now destroyed. Most illustrious and remarkable was the oldest, Sarah Kemble Siddons, with her dark, tragic eyes and tall, striking figure. It has been said of her that she was the greatest actress that ever lived. Her most famous part was the bold and ultimately conscience-stricken Lady Macbeth, but in whatever play she appeared, the old house was always jammed, from the white and gold circle of boxes where sat the aristocrats and prosperous members of the merchant class, to the gallery packed with the boisterous, often unruly poor, who felt the theater belonged as much to them as to their richer brethren.

In 1803, Sarah Kemble Siddons' handsome brother John Philip Kemble had purchased—rather unwisely some felt—a share in the Covent Garden Theatre. He too was a celebrated actor, the most distinguished of his day. Dignified, slow of movement, with fine, classic features he was most suited to patrician roles such as Shakespeare's Julius Caesar or Coriolanus. A scholar as well as an actor, and a man with an independent turn of mind, he had bought the share in the auditorium, risky and uncertain as anything to do with the theater always is, in order to have control over its policies. Since the other owners were businessmen, entirely nonprofessional, the theater, now in smoking ashes, had in a sense belonged to John Philip Kemble. As his wife cried to a close friend who came to commiserate on the morning after the disaster: "Oh Mr. Boaden, we are totally ruined and have the world to begin again."

Six days after the fire, in the true theatrical tradition that "the show must go on," John Philip Kemble mustered his company and staged a production of a now-forgotten contemporary play in another London theater. When the curtain fell a great roar of applause went up not only for his fine acting of the piece but for his gallant spirit. Holding up his hands to quiet the audience, John Kemble in his husky, carefully enunciated way of speaking announced that a new theater would be built at Covent Garden on the site of the old one in the curious location where the air, now that the stench of the fire had cleared, had resumed its familiar market smells of fruit and vegetables—most especially cabbages and onions. So great was the love of Londoners for their theater that money had been quickly raised to build a new and finer one. Among the aristocrats who had contributed to the fund was the foppish Prince of Wales, son to old King George the Third, who had so foolishly conducted the war with the American Colonies a few years before.

It was this stout, ridiculous-looking Prince who laid the cornerstone of the new building on December 30 of the same year the old one had burned. Twenty-one guns roared out a salute to His Highness, who arrived with all his servants in full-dress livery, and when he took up a silver trowel to spread the cement a band began to play. Within the stone were placed various coins and medals representative of the reign of George the Third, and they, together with the stone itself, are preserved in the present theater, which still stands on the same site in Covent Garden.

Within moments the ceremony was finished and the large crowd that had gathered to watch and applaud began to disperse. Among them was Mrs. Siddons, statuesque in a hat with a plume of black feathers; her brother, John Philip, elegantly dressed in blue and white and wearing white silk stockings, and their gentle youngest brother, Charles, just beginning to gain the theatrical experience that would one day link his destiny inextricably with the theater about to be built. How harshly it would treat him—so much so that his as yet to be born daughter Fanny would refer to it as a "terrible millstone" around the neck of the Kemble family—he could not have possibly known.

CHAPTER 2

The Riots

HOUSED IN FILTHY CELLARS, ragged, often hungry, sometimes desperately drunk describes the men who labored to build the new Covent Garden Theatre. Many had been born in the country but had come to London seeking work, now that the invention of new machinery was causing factories to rise in cities all over England. Among the laborers were Irishmen who, because of the unspeakable conditions in their own country, had crossed the rough strait from Ireland to England, looking for opportunity. These men had known such debased standards of living—starvation in mud huts without any possibility of employment whatsoever—that they were willing to work for next to nothing. Since no minimum wage law existed their employers would work them for twelve hours or more at a pay barely enough to keep them alive. All who erected the new theater with the help of the new machinery in the record time of a year were totally uneducated. How could they be otherwise when there were no free schools and their parents had been forced to put them out to work at the age of eight or even less?

Curiously, in this period of English history when there were such terrible deprivations and inequality, no movement developed among the people to revolt—to demand something better. Napoleon, at war with England, had laid plans to invade it. He counted on the down-trodden poor to side with him as their liberator. In fact, historians tell us that every good Englishman would have undoubtedly rushed to repel the foreign invaders of his little island even if the only weapon he possessed were a pitchfork.

Ignorant, brawling, boisterous, the people were much more prone to let off steam among themselves. One place for such release was the theater, and actors as renowned as the Kemble family were accustomed to shouts and even insults from the audience if it was dissatisfied with the play. Sometimes objects were hurled onto the stage when, for example, it was announced that a certain favorite player would not appear. Outside the theater in the real world of the period there were more than 150 crimes, many that would seem to us today very slight, for which a man could be hanged; there was the constant possibility of a man being abducted against his will into the army or navy; and there was always prison awaiting the man who could not pay his debts. But inside the theater with its glow of colors to dazzle the eyes, its exhilaration of words and music and fantastically dressed characters who sometimes seemed more real than life itself, even the most oppressed people felt free.

On the night of September 18, 1809, two days short of a year since the great fire, the orchestra struck up "God Save the King" in the new Covent Garden Theatre and everyone rose to sing it with fervor. A capacity crowd jammed the auditorium, which was slightly larger than the old one but like it, painted white. The decorations were of gold on a light-pink background and in the lovely, glittering chandeliers glowed 270 wax candles. John Philip Kemble had announced *Macbeth* for the opening. With himself in the title role, his sister, the "incomparable" Mrs. Siddons, would play Lady Macbeth, and Charles Kemble was to act Macduff.

There had already been rumors that trouble might break out in the theater that night. But when the National Anthem was concluded, John Kemble with his usual dignity and assurance for which he was celebrated stepped out onto the new, beautifully equipped stage to welcome the audience to the new house. His address, written by himself, was in verse, but as he spoke the first words the noble voice that had thrilled audiences for so many years in great Shakespearean roles such as King Lear, Othello, Henry the Fifth, and Richard the Third could not be heard. From every part of the theater a roar of rage and execration had gone up. Though Kemble read on with amazing self-control, not one line of his speech was heard above the repeated chanting of the furious people: "Old Prices! Old Prices!" Having finished his address, Kemble, with the same remarkable composure, rang up the curtain on the play. Again the shouting and abuse prevented a single speech being heard. Not even the appearance of Mrs. Siddons, the idol of her time, painted by all the great artists and celebrated in verse and prose, could quiet the audience. *Macbeth,* five acts long, was performed by these great actors and not one line of its splendid verse could be heard. So was the new Covent Garden Theatre opened.

The reason for the demonstration was simple enough. A huge sum of money had been raised to build the new theater and, though some of it had been donated outright, most had been borrowed. On this money that was not theirs, the owners, including John Kemble with his quarter share, had to pay interest. The management, therefore, had felt more than justified in raising the prices of admission to certain parts of the house. It was this that had angered the poorer members of the audience. At a time of such tremendous inequality here at last was a place and a cause for demonstrating against their lot.

Then began a siege that lasted for the incredible length of sixty-six evenings. Night after night a play would begin and perhaps the first and second acts listened to in silence. Then the uproar would break out. False fights were staged; people ran up and down the aisles, flailing their arms about in what came to be called the O.P. (Old Prices) Dances. Noisemakers—watchmen's rattles, bells, even a trombone—were smuggled into the theater and made to add to the din. Occasionally the police might evict some of the worst demonstrators, but there were always more and it was virtually impossible to control the large, howling mob.

Through this terrible ordeal the Kembles continued to act with magnificent dignity, though it was obvious that the audiences had singled them out for their most violent demonstrations. Indeed one night a mob laid siege to the London house of John Philip

Kemble. Members of the family might well have feared for their lives. Among these was the charming wife of Charles Kemble, who though almost eight-months pregnant sang and acted the part of Lucy in *The Beggar's Opera* on the night of October 4, 1809. A pretty woman with large eyes and a piquant face, she had always been a great favorite with audiences, especially in pantomimes, though her singing voice was also lovely. That evening as she performed she was pelted by the mob with bitten apples. Stooping somewhat awkwardly for her pregnant state, she collected them and gently threw them off the stage into the wings. Six weeks later the child she had been carrying, a girl who was named Frances Anne, was born on November 27, 1809, while the Old Price Riots continued unabated. Thus did Fanny (as she would always be called) Kemble make her first appearance in a time of violence and dissension.

The issue of the Old Price Riots was clear enough and through the newspapers the various costs of building and running the theater had been made known to the public. If the prices were not raised it would be almost impossible to operate Covent Garden without a loss. But the crowd would not give in. Here at last was a situation in which they had some power to guard their rights, a way of protecting themselves from what they felt to be an injustice. Within the walls of the new theater night after night a tiny little revolution took place and the Kemble family was caught in the center of it.

By December ordinary serious theatergoers, particularly aristocrats and wealthy businessmen who paid the higher prices of admission, would not come to any of the performances since they were inevitably ruined. Finally in the middle of December when Fanny Kemble was less than a month old, John Philip Kemble stepped out on the stage, silenced the audience, and surrendered. The old prices, he said, would be put back.

A cheer went up. Within a second he and his family were once again the idols of London. But John Philip Kemble was still liable for his quarter interest in the theater. This meant that he and the entire Kemble family were now involved with an enterprise that, though it meant their very life to them, could only lose money.

CHAPTER 3

A Question of Acting

A PRETTY, dark-haired child, clever—also willful—Fanny Kemble grew up almost literally in the lap of the theater. One day when she was five and had committed some "crime" to which her Aunt Sarah Siddons was witness, the woman whom Reynolds had immortalized in his painting *The Tragic Muse* hoisted the child onto her lap and began to dress Fanny down in those accents that for years had haunted the ears of the public. When, however, there was a moment's pause in the lecture, Fanny proved a match for the great actress. Looking into her face the little girl said guilelessly: "What beautiful eyes you have." Mrs. Siddons could not keep back her laughter and Fanny was free.

Fanny had her aunt's beautiful eyes as well—dark, dramatic, incredibly expressive. So did another member of the Kemble family who came back from the United States of America during Fanny's childhood. This was her Aunt Elizabeth Whitelock, also an actress. Resembling her sister to a marked degree, she was even larger (not quite six feet tall) and therefore almost a caricature of Mrs. Siddons. Having her sister's manner of speaking and moving, Elizabeth Whitelock had decided it would be more advantageous to make a career on the other side of the Atlantic, where she earned an immense success, even acting before General George Washington and making his acquaintance. Some of her stories of life in the American states seemed to the other members of the Kemble family too incredible to be true. Could there really be roads with ruts and mud holes so deep that carriages sank into them up to their axles? And surely there couldn't be flocks of birds so immense as to darken the sun for a moment?

Aunt Elizabeth Whitelock, Aunt Sarah Siddons, Uncle Stephen Kemble (so fat that he needed no padding to play the portly Falstaff), Uncle John Philip Kemble, her father, her mother—all around Fanny were actors. As her girlhood progressed, one by one, with the exception of her father, they each retired, saying goodbye to their audiences in a poignant farewell speech. Too young to realize yet how the financial problems of Covent Garden were beginning to weigh down her father (for on his retirement John Philip Kemble had given his share in the theater to his brother, Charles), Fanny thus far had known only good from her extraordinary family situation. Actors, writers, musicians, great painters all streamed through her life. References to Shakespeare were constantly on the lips of everyone in the family, and his plays were what nursery stories are to other children. In a time when young girls were scarcely taught more then to read and write, to do needlework, and to play the piano, she thus soaked up an education that was most unusual.

But then the Kemble family were unusual. This is how a certain Captain Gronow, who knew them well, remembered them: "There is not only the stamp of genius and talent of a high order in this gifted family, but also a certain nobility of mind and feeling. . . . No mean thought could make its birth in those broad, grand foreheads . . . and those full, firm, kind lips could not give vent to petty, spiteful or malicious words. They were . . . not of the common clay, but cast in the Titanic mould."

Fanny Kemble's formal schooling, however, was rather sporadic. When very young she was sent to another aunt who lived in the handsome, stylish city of Bath and who ran a "fashionable establishment for the education of young ladies." The education it provided was also fashionable, which is to say practically none at all. Two years later it was decided that Fanny should go to school in France. Mrs. Charles Kemble, Fanny's mother, was after all half French, half Swiss, and it seemed suitable that her daughter should acquire some of her continental background. The school was at Boulogne on the English Channel and here Fanny, always very quick to pick up languages, learned French, a smattering of Italian, dancing, and how to read music. Her willful, independent ways remained as strong as ever, and in that time when the object in raising a child was to break its spirit, her punishments seem terrible to us indeed. Her own parents were not above putting her on bread and water for a day, or locking her in a toolshed to reflect on her sins. But at the school she would be shut up for hours in a black cellar, which her already vivid imagination peopled with all kinds of frightening creatures. Once too, as an example of what could happen to those who were rebellious and attempted to go against the laws of society, she was told she would be taken to witness the beheading of a criminal by the guillotine. Terrified, she was led off to the main square of Boulogne, where the machine had been set up. Whether purposely or not, she never knew, they arrived too late, but the cobblestones of the *place* still ran with blood.

In fact no one ever succeeded in crushing Fanny's stubborn will, her fierce independence of mind, her way of speaking out in a manner that was thought unbecoming in a young lady. It was these traits that made her such a vivid, unusual woman of her time. They were to be her distinction—but also her undoing.

After a year in France Fanny returned home where she did lessons under the supervision of her mother's sister, whom Fanny called Aunt Dall. As an unmarried relative often did in those days, Aunt Dall lived with the family, devoting herself to the children. These now consisted of Fanny's older brother, John; one younger, Henry; and baby sister, Adelaide. In that theatrical atmosphere the four, not unnaturally, began some acting of their own, fitting up a theater with a blue silk curtain that would roll up and even real footlights. For the first time the question must have entered Fanny's mind: might she become an actress? It was, after all, in her blood.

Still largely ignorant of the slow crushing of her father by Covent Garden, Fanny, always remarkably observant, had begun to notice the effect that an acting life seemed to have had on her Aunt Siddons. Now retired, with all the excitement and adulation gone from her life, she seemed dead and indifferent to everything. And wasn't it possible that in always playing theatrical emotions with such intensity (Mrs. Siddons would sometimes faint after one of her performances) it would become impossible to tell the real from the false? How could a person who had acted all her life maintain her sincerity?

When Fanny was twelve and beginning to grow into a not tall, sturdy young woman with flashing brown eyes, her mother took her to another French school, this time one in Paris run by Miss Rowden, an Englishwoman who had a very religious turn of mind. Her girls were made to go to two and sometimes three church services on Sundays, after which they were required to write down what they remembered of the sermons as proof of their attentiveness. Each day they also had to memorize a number of verses from the Bible. Thus Shakespeare and the beautiful prose of the James the First translation of the Bible were the chief influences on the fine, almost sonorous style of writing that Fanny came to develop.

In class she studied geography, grammar, history, arithmetic, and mythology, all taught in French, so that soon she came to think in what was not her native tongue. A feeling for words and language ran through the Kemble family. John Philip Kemble was a scholar of languages, and later, Fanny's older brother, also called John, became one of the great experts on the study of language—philology. When Fanny discovered that only one girl out of all the pupils in the school was learning Latin, she asked to study with her. Together they even mastered the mysterious letters of the Greek alphabet.

Saturdays were given over to instructions in sewing, and Fanny soon became skillful enough to make her own dresses. There was dancing instruction too from a dried-up old man with a beaklike nose who shouted at the girls when they moved awkwardly or forgot their steps, which were taught by the son as the father was too old and infirm to demonstrate them himself. During meals no one was allowed to talk. Instead dry tracts on ethics and religion intended to improve the girls' moral qualities were read out loud to them. On her own, however, Fanny read everything she could lay her hands on: novels, biographies, history, and poetry. One night under the covers she devoured some of the poems of the scandalous Lord Byron that were supposed to be entirely unsuitable for the eyes of a young lady. His poetry affected her then and afterward, she said, "like an evil potion taken into my blood."

Outside the walls of the school was the city of Paris. The girls visited the wonderful cathedral of Notre Dame and many other old churches and walked genteely in the pretty, formally designed garden of the Luxembourg Palace. Inside it, they admired the early nineteenth-century neoclassical paintings of David and Gérard, pleased by their hard, brilliant colors and theatrical compositions.

Best of all for Fanny were the holidays. Instead of returning to her family in England, her father would come to visit her, glad to escape from the hard work and ever-increasing worries that Covent Garden provided. Together they went to restaurants and cafés; they saw the best plays and amused themselves at the variety shows that the French called *vaudevilles*. Fanny had always enjoyed the advantages of a fascinating family background. Now in her three Paris years the world opened up still more for her.

Throughout this time there occasionally must have come to her mind the insinuating question: would she one day become an actress? At Miss Rowden's school the girls were sometimes allowed to put on plays or little *vaudevilles* of their own. Naturally Miss Fanny Kemble always appeared in them. Did not indeed an engraving of her Uncle John in his famous role of Coriolanus hang in the headmistress's study? Most of the parts she acted were slight and frivolous, but finally came the day when it was decided to perform the great tragedy *Andromaque,* by the celebrated French dramatist Racine. Fanny was cast as the jealous, passionate Hermione, who conspires to have the man she loves murdered because he loves another. All the great French actresses had played this part. Style, stage presence, a superb speaking voice were only some of the qualities required to do it justice. Here at last was a challenge, one that would give an answer to the question that had troubled her young life. Would she—*could* she be an actress?

The night of the performance arrived. Everyone who has acted in a school play knows the excitement, the tension of anything to do with it. Fanny's voice had become hoarse with nervousness, and hoping to soothe her throat she swallowed a raw egg that made her sick. Dressed in classic Greek costume, a long white skirt with a short tunic draped gracefully over her shoulders, she walked out onto the stage and began to act. The Kemble intensity, the dramatic Kemble eyes and fine Kemble voice were all hers, and when the play came to its tragic end she felt as electrified by her own acting as the audience seemed to be. Or so she thought.

Backstage, after the applause had died away, Miss Rowden, a friend and admirer of the Kemble family, came up smiling to the flushed and excited young actress. "Ah, my dear," she said wistfully. "I don't think your parents need ever anticipate your going on the stage; you would make but a poor actress."

The question was settled.

CHAPTER 4

The Millstone

FOUR YEARS passed during which the debts of those managing the Covent Garden Theatre continued to mount. Charles Kemble's share of them now amounted to twenty-seven thousand pounds. He was capable possibly of paying five. At one point he thought of selling out and living in the south of France. But who would buy such a liability? The creditors, however, were still willing to let the debts run if they only received a fair return of interest on them. But, with most of the great generation of acting Kembles now retired (all except Charles) audiences failed to crowd into the house the way they used to and often the theater was only half full. What was needed was a star, particularly a woman—another Mrs. Siddons. But where was she to be found?

In the meantime Fanny lived a leisurely life in England, reading constantly (a passion with her) and also attempting literary efforts of her own. These included a historical play called *Francis the First,* which her proud father thought overlong but very good. Her time was divided between the family's house in London near Covent Garden and a little cottage some twenty-five miles south of the city. A huge grapevine grew over the back of the cottage; there were big trees and a lawn. Fanny, who loved the country, would wander over the nearby slopes covered with heather or sit for hours by a neighboring river, her eyes held by the rushing of the water.

There was a piano in the cottage and, besides her writing, Fanny enjoyed singing and playing for herself. She had a good contralto voice, but her mother, who was a professional singer and had exacting standards in everything, thought she didn't sing in tune. It was Fanny's younger sister, Adelaide, with her lovely, accurate mezzo-soprano voice, who seemed to be the real singer in the family.

When Fanny was just over sixteen misfortune struck. Her sister Adelaide came down with the dangerous and disfiguring smallpox. Though innoculations against it were available, Mrs. Kemble had not realized that these must be renewed or the immunity they give wears off. All the children were hastily treated —but too late. Adelaide infected her older sister and her mother as well, though the boys were spared.

When the disease had run its course Fanny looked into a mirror to see that her once pretty features had somehow coarsened. Little marks covered the skin on her face that had once been so clear and lovely. Nothing could change the intensity of her eyes and the vividness of her expression, but she could no longer be said to be pretty. Instead her face took on the odd quality, depending on her mood, of looking either beautiful or plain. No artist who drew or painted her (and there were many) ever caught the same likeness, and sometimes these various portraits seem like those of different people. "Fanny, you are the ugliest and the handsomest woman in London!" an old friend once exclaimed to her.

Soon afterward, Fanny went to stay at the farm of her aunt Mrs. John Philip Kemble, who by then was a widow. Also visiting was a tall, rather mannish-looking woman of thirty named Harriet St. Leger. She wore, Fanny thought, the most peculiar clothes, always gray or black, always very severe. As for her boots, they were exactly like a man's, only uglier. But Miss St. Leger was warmhearted, responsive, and extremely intelligent with a mind full of curiosity about all things. Despite the difference in their ages the two became best friends, and when they parted they agreed to write one another. This they did—for fifty years—sending each other long, full letters, giving every detail of their lives, where they'd been, whom they'd seen, together with a full discussion of the art and literature, the religion and politics of the day. Miss St. Leger, living quietly in Ireland during all this time, saved every one of Fanny's letters and before she died returned them to her. These became the source for the fascinating recollections of her life in three volumes that Fanny Kemble was able to put together when she was a woman in her sixties.

Returning to London, Fanny saw the new opera *Der Freischütz,* which was the rage of the season, by a German, Carl Maria von Weber. The story, a highly romantic one, concerns a shooting contest and a marksman who makes a pact with the devil to obtain a number of magic bullets that will never miss the target. The bullets are cast by the devil's henchman at midnight in an eerie glen, and each time he draws one out with a hiss from the crucible gruesome-sounding invisible spirits repeat his cry: *"Ein . . . Zwei . . . Drei."* The scene chilled Fanny—did it remind her of the terrors of being locked in a black cellar?—and all the rest of the audience as well. The romantic era had begun and public taste demanded plays and operas with wildly emotional characters and situations. Madness was a favorite subject, and the supernatural always welcome.

Weber's opera was such a success that Charles Kemble decided that one way to fill his theater might be to commission another. The famous composer came from Germany to conduct his new *Oberon* personally, and Fanny, awed, met him. Though he was short and plain and frail from the tuberculosis he would soon die of, she placed his picture in a locket around her neck and wore it until the little medal came apart from use.

She had not yet fallen in love. "I cannot swear I shall never fall in love, but if I do I will fall out of it again," she wrote to her friend Harriet St. Leger with all the solemnity of one in her teens pondering this fascinating, if unknown, subject. "I think I should be unhappy and the cause of unhappiness in others if I were to marry."How could she know then that this prophecy of an eighteen year old about herself would come frighteningly true?

That was in February, 1828. The following year Mr. Kemble, who had grown poorer and poorer, finally decided to economize by moving to a little eighteenth-century house with small-paned windows located in Westminster, where Fanny's younger brother went to school near the great stone Abbey. The Kemble family might not be able to afford a horse, let alone a carriage, and all the women in the household might be forced to mend or dye or even "turn" their gowns, wearing them inside out to make them last, but Charles would somehow scrape together the money to send his elder son to Cambridge University and the younger to one of the best private schools in the country. A good education was essential—at least for a man.

One day in September of 1829 Fanny was reading in the living room of the house on James Street, which Mrs. Kemble had somehow managed to make charming even though the furnishings were becoming shabby and worn. She looked up to see her mother enter, sink down into a chair, and—to her amazement—burst into tears. Rushing to comfort her, the nineteen-year-old girl demanded to know what was wrong. "It has come at last," said Mrs. Kemble. "Our property is to be sold. I've seen that fine building all covered with placards and bills of sale; the theater must be closed and I know not how many hundred poor people must be turned adrift without employment."

The long-delayed blow had finally fallen. Covent Garden was to be sold to pay its debts. Hundreds, whose only profession was the theater, not only the actors but also the stage hands, the wardrobe women, the people who maintained the scenery would all be out of work. In that harsh age they could expect no welfare payments from the government. Each person must look out for himself. Not to work, to be poverty-stricken was regarded as, if not actually sinful, a grave fault of character. And what of Charles Kemble himself? If the sale of the theater did not cover the full repayment of his share of its debts, he could be thrown into prison.

A tender-hearted and devoted daughter, Fanny's first reaction to the news was what could she do to relieve her parents from having to support her. What kind of work did her limited education qualify her for? She knew French, some Italian, and had read widely. The answer came quickly to mind. She decided to become a governess. Indeed she liked children and believed profoundly in education. The lack of it in herself—though in fact she was one of those intelligent people who educate themselves—she regretted the whole of her life.

Leaving her mother, Fanny went upstairs to write of her plan to her father, who was touring with a traveling company in Ireland. Dutifully, she showed her letter to her mother and asked if she might post it. Mrs. Kemble agreed, but unknown to her daughter sent word in the same mail to Charles Kemble not to give definite consent to Fanny's becoming a governess until he returned. A clever woman, who all her life had been forced to be resourceful and adaptable, Mrs. Kemble had also formulated a plan.

The next day she stood before her daughter and searched the girl's face and short, almost sturdy figure with her critical eyes. Then in a tone that was oddly meaningful and disturbing she asked if Fanny thought she had any talent for the stage. Bewildered, Fanny could only think back to the one time in Paris that she had ever acted. It was true she had thought that she really gripped the audience. Yet Miss Rowden had said afterward, "Ah, my dear, I don't think your parents need ever anticipate your going on the stage; you would make but a poor actress." Now Fanny suddenly wondered if Miss Rowden with her strong religious bent had really meant what she had said. Could she have recognized the opposite—a great natural acting ability—but tried to discourage it from blooming, out of a religious disapproval of the stage?

To test Fanny's acting talent Mrs. Kemble asked her to learn a part in a play. Favorite of all Fanny's Shakespearean heroines was Portia in *The Merchant of Venice,* her idea of a woman: "wise, witty . . . loving with all her soul . . . a man to whom everybody but herself (who was the best judge) would have judged her inferior." How like Portia Fanny Kemble was to become when she loved such a man, the years would soon show.

Quick at memorizing lines, Fanny recited the part to her mother and breathlessly waited for her opinion. Mrs. Kemble was a critical woman with high standards for all that involved her, whether it was the acting of Shakespeare or cooking. "There is hardly passion in the part to test any tragic power," was all she said. "I wish you would study Juliet for me."

Juliet! The wonderful, dramatic role that most actresses fear to play until they have lived enough years to understand the passion of it! Mrs. Kemble was asking her nineteen-year-old daughter, who had performed only once in a play—and that in French—to undertake this part. Learn Juliet she did, and on the evening of the day her father returned to London (not having given an answer to Fanny's letter about becoming a governess), she recited Juliet to both her parents.

Again there was an odd silence and nothing said that sounded real to the girl's ear, except, "Very well . . . very nice, my dear," and a kiss from her father. What did it mean? Always nervous and high strung, Fanny rushed from the room and sank down on the stairs halfway up to her bedroom in terror and tears.

More days passed in what became for her a torment of suspense. Why did Fanny's parents make no comment on her acting? What was in their minds? One morning she suddenly found out: Charles Kemble asked his daughter to come with him to the Covent Garden Theatre to see if her voice was powerful enough to carry in the large auditorium. For years she had been hearing her family say: if only we could find a successor to Sarah Siddons; if only some great star would appear to bring back audiences to Covent Garden the theater might still be saved. Now Fanny Kemble realized *she was to be the star,* she who was short and unsure of herself, while her Aunt Siddons had been tall and commanding; she who was totally inexperienced in the ways of the stage, while Mrs. Siddons had been the most superb mistress of her art, knowing every cunning trick of movement and voice to win her audience.

Through the market with its jostling, noisy crowds haggling over the price of a pound of potatoes or a head of cabbage, went Fanny Kemble into the vast theater, dark except for a single shaft of light spotting the stage. Within its circle she stood to recite, amid the silent pasteboard and canvas scenery—streets, forests, dining halls, dungeons—stored in the wings. Would her Juliet be as fake as the scenery around her? Would it remain as cold and lifeless as the ink in which the play was printed? Or could Fanny bring to life the strong-willed, passionate girl whose love became her death?

Willfulness, passion, impulsiveness—Fanny Kemble had no need to act these qualities. She was born with them and they remained with her through most of her life. Like Juliet they were to bring her great joy—and tragedy. Recalling that first time she stood on the empty stage of Covent Garden, Fanny Kemble wrote, "My voice resounded through the great vault above and before me, and, completely carried away by the inspiration of the wonderful play I acted Juliet as I do not believe I ever acted it again."

Sitting at the back of the darkened theater, invisible to Fanny, was one of the leading members of London society and a discriminating lover of the theater. At the end of her performance he said simply to Charles Kemble, "Bring her out at once; it will be a great success."

Soon afterward bills went up all over London announcing the reopening of the Theatre Royal, Covent Garden on October 5, 1829, starring Miss Fanny Kemble as Juliet, "being her first appearance on the stage." And so it came about that a raw, not especially beautiful girl of nineteen faced one of the most sophisticated audiences in the world, playing one of the most demanding parts ever written by their beloved Shakespeare.

CHAPTER 5

Debut

THE DRESS, Mrs. Kemble said in her confident way, must be white satin with a long train. Historically it was incorrect. A girl such as Juliet living in Verona in the fourteenth century would have worn something far more elaborate, undoubtedly sewn with jewels. But, argued Mrs. Kemble, Fanny was so very young. Let a simple dress bring out the youthfulness of her figure and leave her free to move comfortably while acting. The girl's acting was the all-important element of this debut, as Mrs. Kemble pointed out with her direct manner: on it Fanny would either fail or become a star.

Three weeks were all the totally inexperienced actress had to learn the "business" of her long role: to which side of the stage she must move on a certain line, when she was to sit, and when to rise again. Her father, Charles Kemble, had always before played Romeo, but now he decided to act the dashing Mercutio, friend to Romeo, since it did not seem appropriate for father and daughter to play the "star-cross'd lovers." William Abbett, a somewhat less than inspired actor, much older than Fanny, was to be her leading man. Vastly reassuring to her was her mother's decision to come out of retirement after more than fifteen years to play Lady Capulet. A real mother would play a stage mother to her daughter.

The day of the performance arrived. That morning Fanny did not rehearse at all but practiced the piano instead and then went for a walk in pretty St. James Park, just opposite her house. To relieve her nervousness she read a highly moral tract called *Blunt's Scripture Characters,* though it is difficult to understand how she could have concentrated on anything so dry.

The play was to begin at seven but the late autumn light was still lingering in the sky over the sprawling city of London as Fanny drove very early to the theater with her mother and father. "Heaven smiles on you, child," said Mrs. Kemble pointing at the lovely light. But Fanny was not so sure. While Mrs. Kemble went to her own dressing room to make herself ready for her part, her sister, she whom Fanny called Aunt Dall, helped the girl to dress and put on her makeup. Seated in a chair with her white satin train carefully laid over the back of it, the realization of what she was about to do overwhelmed Fanny and she began to weep. The tears made stripes along her rouged cheeks, which Aunt Dall, smiling and speaking words of comfort, repainted.

"Miss Kemble called for the stage!" came a cry, followed by a tap at the dressing-room door. Now scarcely knowing what she was doing, she let her aunt lead her around to the wings where half the actors and actresses in the company had gathered to watch her entrance—all except her father, who suddenly could not bear to look. "Courage! Courage, dear child!" one of them said, adding under her breath, "Poor thing! Poor thing!"

"Never mind 'em, Miss Kemble," said a friendly stagehand, whom she had known since childhood. "Don't think of them any more than if they were so many rows of cabbages," he added referring to the audience.

From the opposite wings Mrs. Kemble strode forth to begin the scene:

LADY CAPULET:	Nurse, where's my daughter? call her forth to me.
NURSE:	Now by my maidenhead, at twelve years old,— I bade her come. What, lamb! what, lady-bird! God forbid! where's this girl? what, Juliet!
	Enter Juliet
JULIET:	How now! Who calls?
NURSE:	Your mother.

A tremendous shout went up in the theater as a charming young girl in white satin darted from the wings, ran across the stage, and threw herself into her mother's arms. It was the greeting of a London audience, the most loyal in the world, to this representative of a new generation of Kembles.

JULIET:	Madam, I am here. What is your will?

Nervousness had laid a mist over her eyes and her voice was so tremulous that she could scarcely be heard beyond the front row. The audience waited breathlessly. Would this new Kemble actress with the same dark dramatic eyes of her famous aunt fail to match up to her predecessor? Gradually, Fanny began to lose herself in her part. Her acting became free, her movements almost reckless like those of a headstrong girl madly in love. By the time the Balcony Scene was played she looked radiant, and the passion of the poetry brought blushes to her throat and shoulders. To the enrapt spectators in the theater that night, the small, fiery girl *was* Juliet. And when the curtain fell for the final time an explosion of applause and cheers as loud as any Sarah Siddons had ever received rocked the big, handsome auditorium.

When Fanny came home to supper, exhausted, she found a pretty watch of gold encrusted with jewels beside her plate. It was the first she had ever owned, and, still half a child, she promptly christened it "Romeo" and went to bed with it under her pillow. She awoke in the morning to find herself the toast of London. In one night, just as her parents had hoped, a new Kemble star had risen high over the city. The theater was saved and a whole new life marked out for Fanny—a life that she had never chosen.

CHAPTER 6

Fame

NOW EVERYONE wanted to meet the fabulous Fanny Kemble, transformed as though by magic from an unknown teen-age girl into the most celebrated actress of her time. Plates and saucers were made with pictures of her as Juliet on them. During the nerve-racking weeks of rehearsals before her debut she had sat for the great portrait painter Sir Thomas Lawrence. He was a friend of the family and had wanted to make a drawing of her for the occasion. Engravings of this charming picture now appeared in the windows of many shops, and Fanny saw herself wherever she went in London. Gentlemen wore silk handkerchiefs printed with her picture around their necks and of course she saw those too.

Night after night audiences jammed Covent Garden and applauded her rapturously. With huge receipts at the box office the interest on the debts of the theater could now be satisfied and the sale of the building staved off. Fanny was saving the theater and her family as well. Always intensely critical of herself, Fanny wondered whether her acting really justified all the furore over her. Was she just a passing fashion, young and charming, but little else? Like a dazzling shooting star would she go quickly out of sight? If so, then the theater would go under again.

Yet this is what some of the critics thought of her first performance as Juliet: "Miss Kemble is very young," wrote the critic of the London *Times,* "probably about eighteen, of graceful and well-proportioned figure: her features resemble her mother's but not as much as to be strikingly like her. They are very agreeable and her dark eyebrows and eyelashes, which are extremely handsome, give them a power of expression admirably adapted for the stage. Her voice is flexible and of considerable volume, and her utterance so perfectly distinct that her lower tones are always audible and effective. . . . There was not the slightest portion of awkwardness, or even that want of self-possession which might have been well pardoned in so young an actress. . . . Upon the whole, we do not remember to have ever seen a more triumphant debut."

Said another critic: "For our part, the illusion that she was Shakespeare's own Juliet came so speedily upon us to suspend the power of specific criticism."

And another: "Miss Kemble is a girl of genius."

As for the audience, in their eyes Fanny Kemble could do no wrong. They adored her.

But while Fanny continued to perform, her mother, a fine actress herself and always one to maintain high standards, became more critical of her daughter's playing. "Beautiful, my dear," she would sometimes say, taking Fanny into her arms after the curtain had dropped. But it seemed almost as often that her large, round eyes would snap with anger. "Your performance was not fit to be seen. I don't know how you ever contrived to do the part decently; it must have been by some knack or trick which you appear to have entirely lost the secret of."

Then was she a good actress?

Fanny herself would ponder the question over and over again through the years, concluding with her usual honesty about herself that she was a good actress *sometimes*. With her great dramatic talent and intensity, if the part she was playing interested her and she could really feel it, then she was liable to be marvelous. But if the mood was not upon her, or, above all, if she had to act some of the non-Shakespearean melodramas popular in her day, playing people as unreal as the scenery on the stage, then she felt herself to be uneven—even bad. Her Aunt Siddons had somehow managed to make these unbelievable women come alive and seem real. But Fanny's honesty and literary taste were against her. Only on occasions could she find it in herself to rise above the basic trashiness of these parts.

But for the moment it didn't matter. She was London's favorite, and to this day London audiences are incredibly loyal, refusing to find fault in anyone whom they have taken to their hearts. If one day the novelty of her youth and courageous debut might wear off, there was no use worrying about that now.

Meanwhile there were delightful advantages to fame. Previously her father had managed to give her an allowance of a hundred pounds a year (less than ten dollars a week). Suddenly she was earning 150 dollars a week, a very great sum in those days when the cost of living was low. No longer need she walk everywhere through the muddy London streets. Her earnings paid for a horse and fine carriage and a coachman to drive it. At the age of twenty she was a woman of means, earned entirely by herself, a circumstance most unusual for that time when women were rarely independent and married women had no legal right even to their own property. Fanny had always been independent of manner. Supporting herself so successfully, naturally, did nothing to suppress this aspect of her character.

Another luxury in which she could indulge was horseback riding. She enrolled at the best and most fashionable academy run by a Captain Fozzard, who put her through equestrian exercises designed to improve her seat and her handling of a horse. One day when she was practicing by herself, the riding master appeared in the door of the arena with a middle-aged lady and a very short, rather plain girl. Leaving the women with a low bow, Captain Fozzard came out to Fanny and asked if she would demonstrate some of the exercises he had taught her. Delighted to show off, Fanny put horse and herself through their paces while the two women watched. When she had finished Captain Fozzard returned to the pair and escorted them away. Fanny, always observant, had been struck by his extreme deference to the two ladies. Later she found out the reason. They were the Duchess of Kent and her daughter, Princess Victoria, future queen of England. Well pleased by Fanny's demonstration, the Princess also began to take lessons at the riding academy.

During her first season Fanny acted three nights a week. On those days she would eat a good lunch, usually a mutton chop, in the middle of the day. The play began at seven, but Fanny, escorted by Aunt Dall, would go to the theater long in advance to dress and make up. When she was called to the stage, her faithful aunt (to whom Fanny was devoted) would come with her, holding up the train of her dress so that it wouldn't drag on the dirty floors backstage, and then retire into the wings as the curtain went up. During the intermissions or when she was not in a scene, Fanny quietly did needlework or sewed on a piece of tapestry in her dressing room, her mind occupied with what (usually harrowing) situation she had to enact next.

Very sensitive and high strung as she was, she sometimes immersed herself in the parts she played so completely that she forgot herself. One night while acting in a melodrama that had to finish with a shriek from the distracted heroine, she ran off the stage and down the stairs to the street still uttering scream after scream till she was stopped and brought to her senses. On another occasion while acting the part of a much-put-upon heroine for the first time, her own tears at the plight of this unreal woman overcame her so violently she could scarcely pronounce the words of her part.

Tremendously keyed up by her performances (as is the case with many performing artists), she had difficulty sleeping afterward. The best way of all to relax, she found, was to go to a party, particularly a dance. Since all London eagerly wished to meet her and there was much entertaining in the city, she was showered with invitations.

During her first season she played over 120 performances of Juliet and one devoted fan attended every one, first sitting in various boxes out front, then finally obtaining permission to watch her from the wings. He was, Fanny discovered to her surprise, a vicar. Many in London also knew him to be the illegitimate son of the soon-to-be-crowned William the Fourth. One night she met him at a ball and he breathlessly begged her to dance. She complied, thinking his behavior somewhat odd for a man of the church. Stranger still, when she smiled to someone across the room he instantly asked in a jealous way, "Whom are you nodding to?" then recognizing her father, added, "You're very fond of him, aren't you?"

This too seemed a peculiar question. "I am," replied Fanny in a ringing tone.

"Ah, yes; just so. I dare say you are," said the Vicar in a bitter tone and suddenly burst out in a diatribe against his own father, who would soon be sitting on the throne to which his son could not succeed. Shocked, Fanny said she would not finish the dance with him, whereupon the upset young man apologized and begged her to go on. Fanny, always tender-hearted, relented, and as the quadrille continued the Vicar poured out his woes to her—how he had been trained for a naval career and then forced to go into the church. "You see," he said, "some people have a natural turn for religion; you have, for instance, I'm sure; but you see, I have not." Fanny looked at him sympathetically. "Dear Miss Kemble," went on the extraordinary and evidently much disturbed young man, "will you write me a sermon?"

At this point Fanny, who did indeed have a turn for religion, couldn't decide whether to laugh or be angry. "Certainly not," she said with an attempt at haughtiness. "I'm not a proper person to write sermons and you ought to write your own."

"Yes," said the Vicar humbly, "but you see I can't—not good ones at least."

It was too much for the high-spirited girl, dancing away to the merry strains of a quadrille, and she burst into a fit of laughing. That dance she never forgot.

"Her Juliet is the sweetest I have ever seen," the renowned painter Sir Thomas Lawrence told a friend after Fanny's debut. He had already been attracted by her charms while making his first drawing of her, just as he had been charmed many years before by not one but two of Fanny's cousins, the daughters of Mrs. Siddons, for whom he had declared his love in turn. After Fanny's debut the elegant, almost courtly artist, then in his sixties, asked to draw her again. While he did not talk much as she sat for him, he was moved this time to comment on what gave such special beauty to her eyes. They were emphasized by an unusual double row of long black lashes.

On her twentieth birthday, a month after her debut, Lawrence presented her with a beautiful engraving of Mrs. Siddons as the Tragic Muse, made from a portrait by his fellow artist Sir Joshua Reynolds. On it he wrote, "To her niece and worthy successor." One day after a sitting Fanny sang for him, and the next time he came to the house he brought a song and asked her to learn it. When she sang it for him, this elegantly dressed, usually so reserved gentleman became choked with emotion. What did it all mean? Fanny began to wonder, feeling herself drawn to the painter, even though he was much older than herself.

At every performance she gave, Lawrence sat in the stage box, watching intently, and afterward would sometimes send her a letter offering kind, helpful criticisms of her acting. When the new drawing was finished, he immediately asked if he might make a large portrait in oils of her as Juliet.

Was the great artist interested in her merely as an actress, Fanny asked herself, or as a person in her own right? There is no doubt that she had begun to hope it was the latter.

But Fanny never found out. On the morning of January 7, 1830, when she was actually rereading one of his gentle letters of criticism, her father came to her with the news, "Lawrence is dead." He had died unexpectedly the night before. That evening Fanny had to play Juliet, the part in which Lawrence had so admired her. Filled with sorrow, she wondered how she could go through with it, but, a true Kemble, she went on and acted as though nothing had happened.

It was the one tragedy to mar her otherwise wonderful first year of fame. Being young, she soon recovered from it. But it proved that her heart was perhaps more susceptible than she had thought.

CHAPTER 7

A Time of Travel

IN MAY Fanny's London season ended. Now that she was famous everyone all over the British Isles would want to see her. Charles Kemble took the company on tour—first to the fashionable resort of Bath, where Fanny remembered being "a troublesome brat" at her aunt's school. She acted Juliet to still another member of the Kemble family, her cousin, son of Mrs. Siddons. A strange prudishness had begun to overtake the British with the rise of the middle class, and one of the actors had to lower his voice during a particular speech so that the audience would not hear the reference to "body linen" that it contained. Fanny noticed that her reception seemed less warm than in London. This proved true in a number of cities where she appeared, a fact that she attributed to the fear of the people being thought provincial by slavishly admiring what London admired. The houses were full, however, and that was the main thing.

Coldest of all her audiences was at Edinburgh, where the dour Scots seemed to sit on their hands. There she breakfasted with Sir Walter Scott, who admired her acting as much as she admired his novels. From Edinburgh, on to the fast developing industrial city of Glasgow, where some of the worst slums in Europe were hastily being thrown up. From Glasgow, south again, jouncing along in the crowded coaches that were the only means of transportation at that time. A man named Macadam had invented a covering of crushed stones with which some of the main roads between the large towns were paved, and this made riding a little smoother. But the journeys were still very long and tedious. There was talk of a new invention, the railway, and indeed one was being built between Liverpool and Manchester by gangs of tough, boisterous laborers called "navvies." With the aid of crude machinery, but mainly by pick and shovel, they were hacking deep passageways through rock, building bridges over treacherous ravines, and cutting through forests to lay the tracks for the steam engines that were supposed then to pull strings of coaches connected behind them. The work was incredibly dangerous and many of the navvies were killed in the cause of the "iron horse." But lives at that time were cheap, particularly of these men, a swaggering, fearless lot, rumored to be most immoral when it came to drinking and women. But could a steam engine, which had already done so much to change England from its farm ways to a citified, industrial country, really move a number of people from one place to another?

In July, Fanny excitedly crossed the Irish Channel. Here, in a lovely castle by the sea called Ardgillan lived her friend Harriet

St. Leger, and Fanny was able to visit her. The reunion of the two women, the one tall, drably dressed, the other, now a glamorous actress turned out in the latest and most elegant fashion, might have made an onlooker smile as they embraced. Fanny regretted that Ardgillan didn't look more like a castle, though at least it did have a turret. Best of all was seeing Harriet again, whom she addressed in letters, in the fulsome fashion of the day, as "Beloved."

From Ardgillan she went to act in Dublin, where she received a tremendous reception from the warm and enthusiastic Irish. After one performance her admirers gathered outside the stage door and when she came out someone exclaimed, "Three cheers for Miss Fanny. Bedad she looks well by gaslight."

"Och and bedad she looks well by daylight too!" retorted another fan.

Another night two hundred cheering men escorted her back to her hotel.

Late in August she crossed back over the turbulent channel to Liverpool. In this city, port for the emigrating Irish, living standards among the poor were horrifying. Since the Irish were willing to work for less the only way an English laborer could get work was to accept the same wage. Liverpool had become an important port, receiving cotton shipped mainly from the United States—cotton that had been grown and picked by slaves. However terrible the lot of the English or Irish laborer, at least he was a free man. In Liverpool and other cities great mills were built containing looms that utilized the new steam machinery and helped to develop what became one of England's greatest industries—finished cottons. Supplies of raw cotton from America were vital therefore to feed this burgeoning business from which many people were profiting and helping to make the nation more prosperous. It is said, however, that the average life expectancy of a child born among the working classes of Liverpool at that time was fifteen.

Fanny found the city in a hum of expectancy over the long-awaited opening of the railway, which was to take place next month on the fifteenth of September. The whole idea, backed by the far-seeing merchants and industrialists of Liverpool and Manchester, had been planned by Mr. George Stephenson, a stern-featured man with a dark, deeply marked face. Mr. Stephenson was in fact a good friend of Charles Kemble and on August 25, 1830, invited him and his daughter to take an experimental ride out over the line to a huge viaduct some fifteen miles from Liverpool.

Thus Fanny Kemble became one of the first persons ever to ride on a railroad train, an invention that has done so much to change the face of the earth. Her description of the experience in a letter to her friend Harriet St. Leger has become almost classic, repeatedly quoted by writers of social and economic history. Here are some excerpts from it:

"We were introduced to the little engine which was to drag us along the rails. She (for they make these curious little fire-horses all mares) consisted of a boiler, a stove, a small platform, a bench and behind the bench a barrel containing enough water to prevent her being thirsty for fifteen miles—the whole machine not bigger than a common fire engine. She goes upon two wheels which are her feet, and are moved by bright steel legs called pistons; these are propelled by steam, and in proportion as more steam is applied to the upper extremities (the hip joints, I suppose) of these pistons, the faster they move the wheels. . . . The reins, bit and bridle of this wonderful beast is a small steel handle, which applies or withdraws the steam from its legs or pistons, so that a child might manage it. The coals, which are its oats, were under the bench, and there was a small glass tube affixed to the boiler, with water in it, which indicates by its fullness or emptiness when the creature wants water, which is immediately conveyed to it from its reservoirs."

How carefully Fanny noted every detail of the new invention.

"This snorting little animal, which I felt rather inclined to pat, was then harnessed to our carriage, and Mr. Stephenson having taken me on the bench of the engine with him, we started at about ten miles an hour. . . . You can't imagine how strange it seemed to be journeying thus, without any visible cause of progress other than the magical machine, with its flying white breath and rhythmical, unvarying pace, between these rocky walls which are clothed already with moss and ferns and grasses; and when I reflected that these great masses of stone had been cut asunder to allow our passage thus far below the surface of the earth, I felt no fairy tale was half so wonderful as what I saw."

Like almost everyone of her time, Fanny Kemble held in an almost religious awe the extraordinary new inventions, the wonderful feats of engineering that were threaded through her life and had such an effect on it.

"We had come now fifteen miles, and stopped where the road

traversed a wide and deep valley. Stephenson made me alight and led me down to the bottom of this ravine, over which, in order to keep his road level, he has thrown a magnificent viaduct of nine arches, the middle one of which is seventy feet high, through which we saw the whole of this little valley. It was lovely and wonderful beyond all words."

With the same almost religious awe did Fanny all her life regard nature, particularly mountains—but most of all the hypnotic, entrancing rushing of water.

"We then rejoined the rest of the party, and the engine having received its supply of water, the carriage was placed behind it, for it cannot turn, and was set off at its utmost speed, thirty-five miles an hour, swifter than a bird flies (for they tried the experiment with a snipe). You cannot conceive what the sensation of cutting the air was; the motion is as smooth as possible too. I could either have read or written; and as it was, I stood up, and with my bonnet 'drank the air before me.' The wind, which was strong, or perhaps the force of our own thrusting against it, absolutely weighed my eyelids down."

Fanny left Liverpool to act at Manchester and Birmingham. These were the expanding towns of the Midlands, dismal and dark from smoke and soot that had been created by the industrial revolution. Here she saw and admired the power looms and spinning jennies that were making England, by her enterprise, the most powerful nation in the world. From Manchester she wrote her friend, "Did you know that the solid masses of iron-work which we see in powerful engines were many of them cast in molds of sand—inconstant, shifting, restless sand?" Fanny always had a taste for the paradoxical.

On September 15 the railway was officially opened with the Duke of Wellington in attendance. Fanny, her mother and father had places in the open coaches, together with eight hundred other passengers elegantly dressed for the occasion. Everywhere along the double track line people turned out to see the new "iron horse," to cheer and wave. Fanny felt elated. It was the most exhilarating experience she could ever remember, only slightly dampened by the reaction of her mother, who was certain that traveling at such a terrifying speed must result in instant death.

After an hour the train stopped to take on water, and the directors of the new railroad line got down off their open coach to stretch and walk about. One looked up and saw speeding down on them on the opposite track another engine, without coaches, which was demonstrating its speed. Frantically the men hauled themselves back into their coach—all but one, older and less agile than the others. On the day that England's first important railway line was opened, an engine crushed the leg of one of the enterprising men who had worked to create it. He was taken to a nearby house where he died.

Fanny Kemble, in one of the coaches to the rear, did not see the accident, though the man's shriek, as penetrating as the whistle of the train, silenced all the passengers and spectators alike. But she was present at this the first tragedy resulting from one of the great developments in man's history.

Was it an omen?

CHAPTER 8

The Millstone Again

THAT OCTOBER Fanny opened the new season at Covent Garden once again playing Juliet. A few nights later, while on the very same stage where her mother carrying an unborn child had once been so abused by an audience, for the first and only time in her acting life Fanny heard hisses. They were not for her, however, but expressed the dissatisfaction of the audience with a new play that Charles Kemble had mounted. The passing of the years since the O.P. Riots had done little to temper the passions of people who went to the theater.

The year of the Reform Bill, 1830, was a particularly turbulent time in the history of England, and the public, as usual, seemed to feel free to give vent to their emotions for the price of a ticket to the theater. During this period people had gradually begun to realize that though they had what was supposedly a parliamentary system of government, in fact, the House of Commons where they were represented was controlled by about seventy-five of England's leading families—the aristocrats and landed gentry of the day. Under existing law only people who possessed forty pounds or more worth of property had the right to vote. This left a vast amount of the population disenfranchised. In addition the proportion of representation of the various boroughs that made up England was totally unfair.

A Reform Bill was drafted in the House of Commons to change this unequitable representation, and it was also proposed to reduce to ten pounds the value of property required to vote. The Bill was sent to the House of Lords, and these gentlemen, to preserve their power, vetoed it. In protest, a wave of riots broke out through England and there was talk of revolution.

On the night the Bill was debated for a second time in the House of Commons, Fanny performed at Covent Garden—a benefit for herself. Not even she could draw a full house that evening. As the Parliamentarians argued, crowds demonstrated all around central London, breaking windows and setting fire to effigies with their blazing torches. Such an atmosphere of tension and semirevolution affected the highly strung Fanny, and she remembered in later years how after the curtain had come down she "lay for an hour on my dressing-room floor, with only enough strength left to cry."

The Lords rejected the Reform Bill for a second time but it was returned to them again. As England had grown richer, some members of the working class had begun to educate themselves at night school. Now they demanded the rights inherent in the Constitution but never ceded to them. However downtrodden they may have been, they were free men, not slaves, and had always been aware of their rights; but how to go about achieving them they did not know. With the third reading of the Reform Bill, the House of Lords was forced to submit to the will of the people lest there be total revolution.

Revolution was erupting in many places, including France and Spain. Besides the ever-present worry of the theater, the Kemble family had a new anxiety now. The oldest son, John, had impulsively given up his idea of becoming a clergyman and had run off to help fight the revolution in Spain—one that older and more experienced people could see was a hopeless cause. With him went his friend, the young poet Alfred Tennyson.

Though the violence and uncertainty of the times tended to reduce the size of the audiences at Covent Garden, there was a capacity crowd of elegantly dressed people on the night that King William the Fourth—he who had sired the odd vicar with whom Fanny had once danced—came to one of her performances with Queen Adelaide. The play that night called for Fanny's father to show great anguish and displeasure over her behavior, and even though fully aware that it was all "make believe" she kept confusing her own feelings for him with those of the character she was playing. The idea that her own father, whom she loved tenderly, should show such disapproval of her was almost more than she could bear.

Brighton, that merry, colorful seaside resort, which George the Fourth had made fashionable when he was Prince of Wales, got a chance to see Fanny for the first time in January of the new year.

The house was packed, but she thought her reception rather cold. Her reaction to the town, which she had never seen before, was her usually wildly enthusiastic response to anything connected with the sea and waves. She walked far out of town over the high milky cliffs that border the English Channel and made her way down a dizzying flight of steps. At the bottom, as she wrote to her friend Harriet, "I danced a galop on one smooth little sand island, waited till the tide was coming up, just touched my toe, gave it a kick of cowardly defiance, and then showed it a fair pair of heels and scrambled up the cliff again, very much enchanted with my expedition."

Young and carefree she was at the time and still not burdened by any of the events that were soon to take place in her strange life. There were numbers of delightful dances that year. "I was enchanted with everything," she wrote of one in her diary. "Such shoals of partners! such nice people! such perfect music! Danced until the day had one eye open. The carriage had been ordered for two o'clock, but my father he would not *spoil sport,* so he angelically waited until past four. He is the best of fathers, the most benevolent of men. It is pleasanter to be chaperoned by one's father than one's mother. The latter, poor dear, never flirts, gets sleepy and wants to go home before she comes; the former flirts with every pretty woman he meets and does not care till what hour in the morning." Even so, Fanny regretted that he felt compelled to take her away "in the middle of a delightful mazurka."

With her usual powers of self-analysis, she was well aware of her own immaturity. As England's most famous actress she appeared to be worldly and experienced. But she was not, nor had she ever really suffered (though that would come soon enough). One day she discussed with a friend the question of marriage and a woman's chance for happiness in it. Fanny's view was that some happiness might be gained in marrying but that the risk seemed to her "immense." Her friend looked utterly amazed, and Fanny never forgot the expression on her face—a strange, prophetic moment that she remembered all her life.

Meanwhile, far from suffering, there was a welcome release from anxiety. Word arrived from her brother John in Spain that he was well and safe and on his way home. The revolution, as predicted, had failed. In addition Fanny's historical play *Francis the Frst,* which she had written when she was seventeen, was to be produced at Covent Garden and published in book form as well. There seemed no limits to the success of the brilliant, vivacious Fanny Kemble, just turned twenty-one.

On June 8 of that year a theatrical era passed away. Fanny noted the event in her diary. "While I was writing to Harriet, my mother came in and told me that Mrs. Siddons is dead. I was not surprised. . . . She has been ill and gradually failing for so long. . . . I wonder if she is gone where Milton and Shakespeare are, to whose worship she was priestess all her life—whose thoughts were her familiar thoughts, whose words were her familiar words."

In a way the death of Mrs. Siddons seemed to symbolize the death of the Kemble family's involvement with Covent Garden. Audiences fell off more and more. The debts of the theater mounted again and a number of suits were started against Charles Kemble. One July night when the company was again touring England, Fanny, at dinner with her gentle, aristocratic-looking father, heard him say of one of these suits: "If my cause goes ill before the Lords, I think the best thing I can do will be to take ship from Liverpool and sail to the United States."

America! Fanny could scarcely believe her ears. America! That strange, distant, barely civilized land where her Aunt Elizabeth Whitelock had once told of being followed on a Philadelphia street by an Indian. It was a country, she realized as she thought about it more, that would have no cathedrals, no old abbeys nor ruined cloisters, which were to be seen everywhere in England when she traveled. No monuments to the past of any kind. What a frightening place it must be.

On the other hand the young country was rapidly growing rich. It had no acting tradition of its own and was eager to see the great English players, many of whom, like Fanny's Aunt Whitelock, had gone to the States and come back with sizable fortunes.

"I do hate the very thought of America," she had told her friend Harriet. But she revealed nothing of her feelings to her father, saying simply that she was ready to go with him. Charles Kemble protested that he could not take her from her family and country. He would go alone.

That you never will, Fanny thought in silence.

Returning to London to begin the new season, Charles Kemble was forced to ask the members of his company to accept cuts in their salaries. Weighed down by his financial worries, his health deteriorated: he developed a serious inflammation of the lungs and for day after day Fanny feared for his life, even as she went to the ruinous theater and threw herself into the part that she was acting, still trying to save the very "millstone" that seemed to be crushing the life from her father. Gradually, however, Charles Kemble began to recover his strength. His first thought, characteristically, was when could he act again? None of the members of the older generation of Kembles, John Philip, Charles, Sarah Siddons, ever questioned their lives as actors. The stage was a part of them "like breathing out and breathing in" (as Professor Higgins sings in *My Fair Lady*). It was Fanny, and later her sister, Adelaide, who had what might be described as a love-hate relationship with the theater.

Meanwhile Fanny's devotion to her father and family came first. If there was a fortune to be made in America by her acting, then to America she must go. On February 25, 1832, her mother gave her the news that the luckless fortunes of the theater had again run out. Charles Kemble had fought gamely to save it; so had his daughter by accepting a profession that she never entirely approved of. Now at last the theater was lost.

Fanny had been reading and crying over a novel by James Fenimore Cooper, and her eyes were hot and aching. Ironically, her imaginary sorrow became real. "I wonder if any country is more blessed of God than this precious little England?" she had written to her friend Harriet the previous summer. Now she must leave it. Without responding to the news her mother had given her, she went to the window and looked up and down the London streets that at that hour were becoming empty and dark and silent—and her heart sank.

There still remained the season to finish followed by a short tour before the evil day of departure would arrive. That spring,

Fanny's play *Francis the First* was successfully produced at Covent Garden. Fanny, as usual, more critical of herself than anyone else, thought it empty and lifeless and believed that audiences crowded the theater only because it was written by a seventeen-year-old girl with the authoress, now all of twenty-one, playing a leading part.

May came on, one of England's loveliest months. Trees bloomed and leafed out in the London parks and flowers began to appear in the window boxes of houses. But for Fanny there was a sad round of farewells. From her friends she received sentimental tokens to commemorate the leave-taking as was the fashion of her day. From her devoted audience at Covent Garden came a tremendous ovation that made her burst into tears and sob wildly as she left the stage—never, in fact, to act on it again.

More leave-takings occurred beside the Thames at Greenwich out of which Fanny sailed with her father up the North Sea to Edinburgh, where she was to perform. Goodbye to older brother John, now returned home from Spain, just as she, ironically, was going off; goodbye to her remarkably handsome younger brother, Henry, and goodbye to "baby" Adelaide, now grown much taller than Fanny and the possessor of a lovely singing voice. They were an exceedingly close-knit family. When would she ever see them again?

At Edinburgh, the Scots were their usual chilly selves when it came to applause, but the attendance was good. Once, in her teens, Fanny had made a long and happy visit with a relative in this dramatic looking city. Now every stone of it seemed precious to her. Here took place the worst farewell of all—with her mother, who had to go back to London to look after Henry and Adelaide, replacing Aunt Dall who was then to join Fanny at Liverpool and also sail to America. Aunt Dall was sacrificing herself to play the indispensable role of chaperon to her niece.

Fanny reached Liverpool toward the end of July. She thought the city with all its important wealth and industry "a dismal looking place, a swarming world of dingy red houses and dirty streets." Awaiting her arrival was her "beloved" Harriet St. Leger, who came especially from Ireland to say goodbye and to bring a drawing to Fanny of herself that she had commissioned so that her friend would not forget how she looked.

On August 1, 1832, the clipper ship *Pacific* hoisted sail and began the long crossing to the New World.

Fanny, though she could not know it, would never have a family home of her own in England again.

CHAPTER 9

First Impressions

JUST OVER a month later, the *Pacific* swung helplessly becalmed outside the narrow entrance to New York Harbor with the city tantalizingly out of view from the ship. The length of the voyage had been considered unusually short, though not enough to mitigate the dullness of it for one as high spirited as Fanny. She spent the tedious days reading, doing needlework and embroidery, and keeping up her journal, though there wasn't much to record in it. "I want to do everything in the world that can be done, and by the by that reminds me of my German" (which she was teaching herself), she commented in its pages. Idleness—physical or mental —was not in her.

When a storm had struck the little boat, reading, German, and journal writing stopped abruptly for a number of days. But after the seas subsided slightly Fanny went out on deck and let the tossing waves hypnotize her eyes while the wind roared in her ears and whipped her long dark hair across her face. There, she reflected on eternal things, God and the creation of the universe, the imponderable stars glittering in the black summer sky, and the infinite stretches of water spread around the rocking ship. Below, in her cabin, lay poor Aunt Dall, who had so generously sacrificed herself to come to America and who was sick throughout the entire crossing.

Now, hour after hour, the *Pacific* continued to dawdle, adding to the already extreme anxiety of some of the passengers aboard. A passing ship had given news of a severe cholera epidemic in New York City that was daily taking the lives of many people. Were their own families safe, these passengers wondered. Those New Yorkers who could had fled the dreaded disease to isolated areas in the country. Until the epidemic passed, there would be no audiences to witness the brilliant acting of Charles Kemble and his famous young daughter, Fanny.

When the wind finally picked up and the *Pacific* was able to sail through the Narrows into New York Harbor, Fanny could at last view the busy port city with that intense curiosity she brought to all things new to her. In 1832, New York City still took up only the southernmost part of Manhattan Island. To the north, at Murray Hill, for example, where the Empire State Building now stands, there was a farm. Nonetheless, the city had grown so quickly since colonial days that it had become too big for the existing municipal conveniences. There were no water mains, and water had to be delivered to houses in huge barrels. Pigs, roaming the streets, were the chief garbage collectors of the day, and paper and dust off the unpaved streets blew about in the wind. Fanny, however, thought the city looked a little like Paris mainly because the houses all had shutters and because it was "very gay, rather like a fair."

To her delight she found a piano in her hotel room and pounced on it, having had to do without playing and singing throughout the long sea journey. The cholera epidemic had indeed been very severe but was now diminishing according to the mysterious pattern it always assumed, and people were beginning to return to town. The Kembles, it was decided, would make their first appearance in two weeks time at the attractive Park Theatre, conveniently situated near their hotel, both buildings in fact facing New York's handsome City Hall, which still stands today.

Mr. Kemble left letters of introduction with a certain Mr. Philip Hone, a former mayor of New York and a cultivated person who loved the theater and music. As was the custom of the day, Mr. Hone politely replied by calling at the hotel in order to ask the Kembles to dinner. Fanny sent down word that her father was out, but Mr. Hone, fascinated to meet her, having heard so much about her, insisted upon coming up anyway. In walked, as she recorded in her diary, "a good-looking elderly man," elegantly dressed, "one of *the* men of New York, in point of wealth, influence and consideration." Mr. Hone also kept a diary, to which he commented on Fanny: "She appeared deserving of all her reputation: a good figure, easy manners, sprightly and intelligent, self-possessed, not very handsome, but with animated and expressive features, and calculated for great stage effect."

Everyone wanted to meet her. A young man with an introduction asked if he might call and bring a friend. When Fanny consented he showed up with three others—four fine young men all eager to pay her court. Of their conversation and general behavior, she thought sniffily, if these were American manners "defend me from them."

In fact during her first days in New York she was highly critical of this young, still raw city and the people who lived in it. When she went to dine with Mr. Hone he thought her manners "singular" and noted that, unlike most women of his day who were excessively and submissively polite, Fanny made no effort to talk to anyone who did not interest her. Mr. Hone had seated her next to himself and, fortunately, found himself in her favor. Then she talked with such fascination and charm that, as he expressed it in his journal, he "lost his dinner to her" by listening and forgetting to eat. Shrewdly he noted that the theater was not her favorite theme of conversation. "I am of the opinion that she does not like her profession."

After dinner she played and sang for the company. "Her voice is not sweet, but has great force and pathos." The eagerness of the courteous, kindly gentleman to see Miss Kemble act became further whetted. "I am confirmed in my opinion that she possesses astonishing requisites for the stage."

Fanny's comments on the dinner party in *her* diary were rather different. The dinner was "ill-served; there were not half servants enough; no water glasses, no finger bowls." She was scornful of the naïveté of her other dinner partner, and, after the meal when asked to sing, was annoyed that the small parlor piano faced the wall. The fact is—as often remains the case with English people to this day—she was taken aback by the difference in manners outside her own country, particularly in a civilization as new as the American one. The English way was the right way, and the difference and strangeness of everything in the United States, while it fascinated, also frightened her.

Because of the lack of a water system in the city, with most of the houses made of wood, there were half a dozen fires every night and firemen "tearing up and down the streets, accompanied by red lights, speaking trumpets and a rushing, roaring escort of running amateur extinguishers who make night hideous with their bawling and bellowing." One night there was a tremendous storm with "great forked ribbons of fire" and "deep full-toned rolls that made the whole air shake and vibrate with the heavy concussion." She was homesick too. She watched a wonderful sunset over the Hudson River filled with glowing colors unlike anything she had ever seen in her own country and thought she would have given it all—gold and glorious purple—"for a wreath of English fog stealing over the water."

In the interests of good showmanship Charles Kemble decided to make his first New York appearance as Romeo without his daughter. Two nights later Fanny would then appear playing without her father. Only after this would audiences be given an opportunity to see the great pair act together. On September 17, 1832, Charles Kemble made his New York debut while Fanny sat out front in a turmoil of anxiety. What would these rough, inexperienced people, totally ignorant of theatrical traditions think of her father's sensitive, subtle interpretation of Shakespeare? She need not have worried. When the curtain came down there was an immense ovation while tears of relief and happiness rushed into Fanny's eyes. Always prepared to find fault with American ways, however, she noted in her diary the way the public had received her father: "They should see our London audiences get up and wave handkerchiefs and shout welcome as they do to us."

Fanny's turn came two nights later. She was in her usual nervous state, made much worse by the realization at rehearsal that her leading man provided by a local New York acting troupe was a hopeless actor and did not even know his part. Too frightened to take her whispered promptings (for she knew his lines as well as her own) the only thing that poor Mr. Keppel could think to do was to go down on his knees, "which he did every five minutes," as Fanny wrote in her comic way to Harriet St. Leger of this, her New York debut. "Once when I was on mine, he dropped down suddenly opposite me and there we were, looking for all the world like one of those pious conjugal *vis-à-vis* * that adorn antique tombs in our cathedrals. It really was exceedingly absurd."

Yet somehow she managed to save what was supposed to have been a tragedy from becoming a farce and made a triumph, if anything, greater than her father's. "I have never witnessed an audience so moved, astonished and delighted," commented Mr. Hone. "Her display of the strong feelings which belong to the part was great beyond description, and the expression of her wonderful face would have been a rich treat if her tongue had uttered no sound. The fifth act was such an exhibit of female powers as we have never before witnessed, and the curtain fell amid the deafening shouts and plaudits of an astonished audience."

As in London, in one night Fanny Kemble had become the talk and the toast of New York.

* People face to face.

CHAPTER 10

Fame Again

"WE HAVE SEEN the finest female genius the stage at this day has to offer," trumpeted the critic of one newspaper following Fanny's first New York appearance. As the darling of the city, huge (and to Fanny's thinking) extravagant bouquets of flowers arrived constantly at her hotel. Young men called upon her and sometimes she went horseback riding with them up Broadway or to places such as Lenox Hill—chaperoned, of course, as always by faithful Aunt Dall. Hundreds of people wanting tickets for her performances had to be turned away, but one who saved up his pennies and traveled over from Brooklyn was thirteen-year-old Walt Whitman, who managed to see Fanny Kemble several times. "Fanny Kemble . . . Nothing finer did stage ever exhibit," the poet recalled later, "the veterans of all nations said so and my boyish heart and head felt it in every minute cell. The lady was just matured, strong, better than merely beautiful—born from the footlights—had had three years' practice in London and through the British towns; and then she came to give America that young maturity and roseate power in all their noon, or rather forenoon, flush." Her performances together with those of one or two other great actors and singers Whitman claimed gave him the inspiration for the first part of *Leaves of Grass.*

Fanny's acting influenced another young person so strongly that she decided to embark on a stage career of her own. This was the famous American actress Mrs. Mowatt. "Never have I beheld any creature so perfectly bewitching," she remembered of Fanny's performances. "The tones of her voice were richest music, her dark flashing eyes seemed to penetrate my soul and I laughed and wept immoderately."

But if Fanny was New York's darling, New York was not hers. By now she was used to fame and adulation; indeed it almost wearied her. Meanwhile she continued to complain petulantly to her diary how rude the tradespeople were, how there were never enough servants and that the carriages were ugly and slung dangerously high. As for the extremes of weather, boiling one day, freezing the next—they were not to be borne. She did admit, however, that the light of the New York sky—a city, it will be recalled, that is on a far more southern latitude than London—was most beautiful.

The general lack of cultivation among people whom she met also bothered her. On the other hand she observed correctly that there were no such poor and down-trodden as had always surrounded her in England. Returning from an excursion across the Hudson River in the lovely woods at Hoboken, she joined a throng of well-dressed, well-fed men—laborers, tradespeople, artisans—with their families, all of whom looked happy and filled with well-being. But, Fanny asked herself, what about the happiness of more cultivated people like herself? "Where are the picture galleries—the works of art and science—the countless wonders of human ingenuity and skill? . . . A race in a circular railroad car or a swing between the lime trees" was not enough. "Where are all the sources from which I am to draw my recreations?" Of course she was right. America was too young to have developed much in the way of artistic resources. Indeed Fanny's tremendous success in the new country can partly be attributed to this lack.

One other evil distinction she became aware of between life in London and New York. The boat she had crossed on, the *Pacific,* was still tied up at one of the New York piers and one morning the steward, a Negro, came to the hotel to ask Charles Kemble for a ticket to a performance. It would have to be a seat in the balcony, he added. Black people were not permitted to go into any other part of the theater. Could this be true in democratic America, especially in the North, which had renounced slavery unlike the Southern part of the country? Had not Thomas Jefferson declared that in this new nation every man was born equal in his right to life, liberty, and the pursuit of happiness?

Soon afterward a friend called on Fanny and in the course of their conversation began to speak of a trip he had made to the South. He told her how he had seen slaves being whipped in the fields, and tears sprang into Fanny's eyes. She herself came from a country where flogging was a commonplace punishment for criminals, for men in the army and navy—and in a slightly less drastic form for schoolboys. Her indignation and pity stemmed far more from the fact that the men were slaves. Her existence in England had exactly paralleled the time when a national movement against slavery in the English colonies such as Jamaica had begun to mount. Though no woman in England had the right to vote, women nonetheless had organized petitions with thousands of signatures protesting slavery and had sent them to Parliament. However crushed in other ways the poorest English citizen had ever felt, there was always a feeling of independence in him; indeed that very spirit had caused many Englishmen to seek greater freedom in the new land of America when oppression in their own country had seemed too intolerable. Curiously, in 1833, one year after Fanny Kemble first came to America, Parliament finally abolished slavery in the English colonies.

This English agitation against the evil practice seemed now to cross the Atlantic with her and antislavery societies began to grow up in large Northern cities such as New York and Philadelphia. One year before Fanny had landed in New York, an obsessed crusader with angry, protruding eyes named William Lloyd Garrison founded a Boston paper, *The Liberator,* in which he printed brutal and horrible accounts of atrocities committed by slave owners on their bondsmen. He and a number of men who became the rabid abolitionists of the day possessed all the zeal of religious fanatics. In that moral, pious time, a man's Christian duty was held to be that of saving his fellow men from sin. And these men were convinced that holding slaves was a terrible sin indeed.

Naturally the Southern slave owners found this message from

Northern busybodies scarcely welcome, though it is true that a number of men who kept slaves did have troubled consciences about it. These qualms could be held in check, however, by reference to certain passages in the Bible that declared that the holding of one race in bondage by another was God's word. Above all, they denied the accusations of the "Garrisonites"—as some of the more vehement abolitionists came to be called—and claimed that they treated their slaves most humanely, feeding and clothing them, and tenderly taking care of the very old and the newly born. Continuing the practice of slavery, argued the plantation owners, was their sacred duty, for what would happen to these ignorant, childlike people—several million of them—if they were freed and turned loose on the country? This was a thought that people with more moderate antislavery views could not help but ponder.

Some of the most extreme abolitionists, believing it to be their sacred duty, would sometimes go into a Southern town or onto a plantation and attempt to preach against the sinfulness of slavery. As often as not these men were tarred and feathered and run back to the North.

With so much vehemence on the part of both sides it was puzzling for people of more moderate or mixed views to decide what was the truth. A few accounts of slavery in the nineteenth-century American South had been published by foreign visitors. One of them, a trenchant Englishwoman named Harriet Martineau, much admired by Fanny Kemble, had little use for slaveholding in general, but noted that "The thoughtfulness of masters, mistresses and their children about, not only the comforts, but the indulgences of their slaves, was a frequent subject of admiration with me." But Miss Martineau's impressions were slight and superficial. Urgently needed was a closely detailed account, a "record" of life on a typical slave plantation by someone intelligent, observant, and possessing the power to write.

Meanwhile, to Fanny Kemble, newly arrived in America (and adjusting to it rather poorly), slavery seemed fairly remote. She was an Englishwoman and loathed the idea of slavery. But there was no need for her to bother with the problems of this rough-and-ready country. Her business was to act.

On October 8 at a quarter to five in the morning Fanny hoisted herself out of her New York hotel bed with a groan. She and her father were to play an engagement in Philadelphia and the boat that was to take them on the first lap of their journey left at six. This was the life of a trouper. She was amazed to see that a friend had also gotten up to help them off at that dismaying hour. If Americans were not cultivated at least they were kind.

The boat took them down New York Harbor past Staten Island to Amboy, at that part of New Jersey where the state is narrowest. Here Fanny climbed into a waiting stagecoach suspended high above its wheels. Five other passengers plus some of the Kemble paraphernalia that would not go into the trunks, such as bulky capes and cloaks, were crammed into the stuffy carriage and off it started. Though America had paved turnpikes linking various Eastern cities as early as 1800, its side roads were usually made of trees felled across the track and the trimmed trunks lined up side by side. These were called "corduroy" roads. Fanny thought the one in New Jersey "the cruelest, hard-heartedest that ever wheel rumbled upon." Roots of the felled trees stuck up along the way and boughs scratched the jolting, shaking, bumping vehicle as four horses drew it relentlessly along. One of the passengers was sick throughout the journey. Sometimes they went through a muddy place where the wheels sank almost to their axles, and Fanny might well have remembered—with some bitterness—how all the family had disbelieved Aunt Whitelock's stories of life in America.

Fourteen miles later came release. The Kembles transferred to a railway train, but different from the one that Fanny had ridden at Liverpool in that the cars were horse drawn. America was slightly behind England in the introduction of the steam locomotive, though it was just then beginning to come into use. Steamboats, however, were common—thanks to the commercial success of Robert Fulton's *Clermont* launched in 1807—and Fanny found one waiting for her on the banks of the Delaware to which the railroad had brought her. The width of the river amazed her, and the boat for once pleased her by the comfort it provided. It had an additional virtue: smoking was forbidden, though not that other abomination—spitting. Everywhere she went in America everything was covered with the spewings of chewed tobacco: streets, stairs, backstage, and even on the stage itself. Supposed "gentlemen" thought nothing of spitting on the carpet in a house.

At four o'clock she arrived in Philadelphia, a distance of not quite a hundred miles accomplished in the amazing time of ten hours. She immediately liked the city better than New York. It seemed to have an "older," more stable atmosphere. Here, where American liberty had been born, Fanny met her destiny.

CHAPTER 11

A Mysterious Admirer

"OCTOBER 30, 1832. . . . The Philadelphians are about the most inhospitable people it was ever my good fortune to fall in with," wrote Fanny adding a new kind of complaint to her journal. As in New York, Charles Kemble had made his first appearance in Philadelphia to great acclaim, followed by Fanny on her own two nights later. Henry Wikoff, a young man about town (and there were many in rich Philadelphia society), was present at her debut and remembered afterward: "Her first appearance impressed and delighted the house. . . . When she spoke her rich resonant voice captivated every ear. Her bearing and attitude were so natural and withal distinguished that the audience was half won before she essayed to act.

"But when she rose with the action of the play and began to display her power—when she gave to the fierce passions of the role the agonized threats of the half-maddened wife—the spectators were transported with enthusiasm and wept and applauded wildly by turns. That single performance stamped Fanny Kemble to my mind as the greatest of living actresses, and it has never been effaced from my recollection."

Fanny, on the other hand, thought the audiences abominably cold: they did not even applaud her famous and beautiful Balcony Scene when she played Juliet. She did admit that the ovations after the final curtain were immense. Still further proof of her success came from the box office in front of which men actually brawled and fought to get tickets. Every night the house was sold out. With all the excitement over her, a Philadelphia publisher asked if she would write something, anything, for him. Fanny demurred but her father, believing that publicity would be useful, urged her to provide the man with something. Fanny had always been in the habit of writing poems mostly about nature, and she offered two on autumn to the publisher, Mr. Carey, who promptly printed them in his newspaper. One began:

> The merriest time of all the year,
> Is the time when the leaves begin to fall,
> When the chestnut trees turn yellow and sear
> And the flowers are withering one and all.

It finished on a still more sour note that seemed to reflect her unhappiness with her fatiguing life as an actress in a strange country. Of course what the public would really like, Mr. Carey pointed out, would be some of the famous actress's impressions of America. Could she not set some of them down? Fanny had already done exactly that every day in her journal—but these views and comments, as she pointed out to him, would be much too personal to print. What if blanks were substituted for all the names of people she had mentioned, suggested the publisher. Surely no one would mind, nor even recognize themselves. Fanny stood firm. His offer would always be good, Mr. Carey reminded her, in case she changed her mind.

Night after night she thrilled Philadelphia: audiences cheered and roared their approval and afterward hung about the stage door until she appeared, carefully chaperoned by Aunt Dall or her father. Yet few people, as she had noted in her journal, came to call or asked to meet her, a situation completely different from New York, where the Kembles were asked out constantly. What was wrong?

The answer, as Fanny correctly felt just by the "sense" of the town, was that Philadelphia had an older, more conservative tradition than mercantile New York. People in Philadelphia were not so busy laying up money; they already possessed it, often through holding vast tracts of land in other parts of the country. This meant that the society was a more aristocratic one, concerned with names and family position—indeed very much like the society that Fanny had left in London. Ruled by more snobbish standards it is not surprising that Philadelphia did not at first open its doors to Fanny Kemble or her distinguished father. After all, they were *actors*.

Fanny's charms, however, were sufficient to break down the reserves of a number of young men from these fine aristocratic families. Among them were Edward Biddle and Pierce Butler. The latter, blond and very good looking, appealed to Fanny because he seemed intelligent, well read, and loved all the arts including music. He could even play the flute. Pierce Butler was already wealthy, and, though by profession a lawyer, he did not practice, which gave him the leisure to go riding with her or accompany her on shopping tours. When an old aunt of his died he would be very rich indeed, Fanny had been informed, though she was not told the source of this tremendous wealth. For his part Pierce Butler was fascinated by Fanny and never missed a performance when she acted. This was nothing new to an actress used to the worship of fans. Nonetheless his attentions were particularly welcome at a time when there was something of a dearth of social opportunities. It was Pierce Butler, too, who introduced her to his cousin, the artist Thomas Sully, who immediately asked if he might paint her portrait, which Sully did several times.

More intriguing to one of Fanny's dramatic and romantic disposition was the arrival one day of a lovely bouquet of flowers with a card signed simply, "From a Philadelphia *friend.*" Did the underlining of the word "friend" mean "Quaker"? Or was it some old friend, perhaps from England, who had arrived in Philadelphia and was about to surprise her with a call? Two days went by and the mystery deepened. She came in from a walk along the banks of the Schuylkill River during which her eyes had felt drunk with the colors of the sky and landscape and found another bunch of flowers from the unknown "friend." What did it mean? They must be from some admirer, but why didn't he make himself known to her? The flowers continued to arrive and Fanny became more and more mystified. Who could the person be? What was he like?

Whether Philadelphia society offered her invitations or not, what with the flattering attentions of Mr. Butler, Mr. Biddle, and Mr. Sully—not to speak of the regular delivery of the bouquets—Fanny's spirits began to lighten. Perhaps she was simply getting used to American ways and American manners. Certainly the young country had begun to interest her for she read a history of it and was much impressed by how the United States had been founded. Her father, Aunt Dall, and Fanny went to Liberty Hall to see the building from which Thomas Jefferson's Declaration of Independence had been proclaimed. It set her mind to thoughts about England's loss of the American Colonies less than sixty years before, a fact that many in her native land still deeply regretted. Perceptively, Fanny came to the conclusion that even if England's treatment of the Colonies had been far more generous and lenient, the separation had been inevitable. America was a land too enormous and with too many resources not to insist upon its eventual independence.

"Far from regretting that America has thrown off her allegiance," she wrote in her journal, ". . . England will surely, ere long, learn to look upon this country as the inheritor of her glory; . . . Loving and honoring my country as I do, I cannot look upon America with any feeling of hostility. I not only hear the voice of England in the language of the people, but I recognize in all their best qualities, their industry, their honesty, their sturdy independence of spirit, the very witnesses of their origin, they are English; no other people in the world could have licked us as they did; nor any other people in the world built upon the ground they won, so sound, so strong and fair an edifice."

Then with the strange talent for historical prophecy that Fanny possessed, she added of the United States: "Such numerous and clashing interests, such strong and opposite individuality of character between the Northern and Southern states; above all, such enormous extent of country . . . tell against the probability of its long remaining at unity with itself."

On the fifth of November at five-thirty in the morning Fanny again wrenched herself from bed and dressed by candlelight. Travel was the remorseless lot of theater people: the Kembles were returning to New York for another engagement. She regretted leaving Philadelphia. Even though the audiences seemed to her intolerable in their coldness—and society too, for that matter—she liked the city. There was something about its stability, its atmosphere of tradition that reminded her of England. She would be leaving too her circle of admirers, whom on evenings when she wasn't acting she liked to receive and entertain by singing for them. More persistent than the others, Pierce Butler asked if he might come to New York and call on her there. He suggested that on a day when she was free they make an outing up the Hudson River to West Point and the spectacular Storm King Mountain that looms high above the river. Laughingly she agreed, amused by his intensity—something she had seen over and over in many a fan who had come to worship. She had one more regret at leaving Philadelphia: now she would never know who the mysterious admirer was who had sent her flowers.

Returning to New York Fanny found the city cold, gray, and melancholy. As usual there were the never-ending chores of her profession to be performed, unpacking, mending, and putting away all her costumes, as well as making new ones which she usually did herself. She also had to keep her own clothes looking fresh and attractive; the off-stage appearance of an actress was important. Three days after leaving Philadelphia Fanny was sitting in her hotel room retrimming a green velvet bonnet, "a worthy old thing" that still looked amazingly well, when she received a welcome call from Pierce Butler. He had come to New York and hoped very much that Miss Kemble, Aunt Dall, and Mr. Kemble would make the outing to West Point on the following Saturday if the weather was fine.

That night Fanny performed in a dress as red as a bonfire to a crowded house and thought afterward that she had given a fine performance. Elated, she walked home by the light of a full moon that flooded the city with its cold rays, and opening the door of her hotel room, stopped on the threshold. There, before her, almost as large as herself, was a basket of autumn flowers—dahlias, Michaelmas daisies, pungent-smelling chrysanthemums. The card was signed in the same handwriting from her "Philadelphia *friend*."

Then who was he? Why wouldn't he reveal himself to her? Was he in New York? Perhaps he had even followed her there purposely. Of course Pierce Butler had come to New York that very day. . . .

Pierce Butler?

Now that she thought about it, out of the various young men

who had ever paid her court, he seemed far and away the most sincere, the most truly devoted. The others pretended to be, but she knew that was nonsense, a game they played to gain admission to the circle of the most famous actress in America and England.

But Pierce Butler?

Of course the whole business did not really bear thinking about. Even if his affections were more than a little serious, hers were not and never could be. True, Pierce was charming, sophisticated and very handsome. She enjoyed his company very much. But more than that . . . And then came an even more arresting thought: the whole idea of treating him seriously was ridiculous. After all Pierce Butler was *American*.

CHAPTER 12

"I Shall Never Fall in Love"

AGAIN AUNT DALL was shaking her awake in the dark of the morning. It was the following Saturday and, as Fanny grumpily dressed herself by the usual light of a candle, she thought that this was scarcely her idea of a day of pleasure. This time she was not going off to act in some other city, but catching a boat for the outing up the Hudson River. By eight o'clock, having passed the Palisades, the sun had come out and Fanny's spirits began to rise, as "rock and river, earth and sky shone in intense and dazzling brilliancy. The broad Hudson curled into a thousand crisp billows under the fresh north-wester that blew over it."

Enthralled, the little group stood on the deck of the boat moving up the river at fifteen miles an hour—Aunt Dall, Fanny with Pierce by her side, and another older man, a colonel, talking to Charles Kemble. They passed the woods of Sleepy Hollow and the "marble prison of Sing Sing," then crossed the Tappan Zee where the great river widens out into an enormous basin. Fanny grew more and more excited by the beauty of it all.

"The giant shadows of the mountain on the left, falling on the deep basin at their feet, the triumphant sunlight that made the restless mirror that reflected it too bright for the eye to rest upon, the sunny shores to the right, rising and falling in every exquisite form that hill and dale can wear, the jutting masses of granite, glittering like the diamond rocks of fairyland in the sun, the golden waves flinging themselves up every tiny crevice, the glowing crimson foliage of the distant woods, the fresh vivid green of the cedars that rifted their strong roots in every stony cleft and threw a semblance of summer over those November days—all, all was beautiful and full of brightness."

At a quarter to eleven they left the boat and climbed the steep path that led to the buildings and parade grounds of West Point Military Academy. Above them on top of Storm King Mountain was Fort Putnam, built during the Revolution to defend the river from Fanny's own countrymen. With an hour left until dinner time the party decided to climb up to it. Fanny had not sat down once while aboard the boat in her excitement at the wonders of the scenery and had supposed she was tired. But now as they started to climb, a strange wave of exhilaration came over her, sweeping her on faster and faster until she was out of sight of the rest of the group.

"Through close growing trees and shrubs, over pale, shining ledges of granite over which the trickling mountain springs had taken their silvery course, through swampy grounds where the fallen leaves lay like gems under the still pools that here and there shone dimly in little hollow glens. Over the soft, starry moss that told where the moist earth retained the freshening waters, over sharp, hard splinters of rock and rough masses of stone. . . . Happy [I] went on my way rejoicing, climbing and climbing still, till the green mound of thick turf and ruined rampart of the fort arrested my progress. . . . I looked down and for a moment my breath seemed to stop, the pulsation of my heart to cease—I was filled with awe. The beauty and wild sublimity of what I beheld seemed to crush my faculties—I felt dizzy as though my senses were drowning—I felt as though I had been carried into the immediate presence of God. Though I were to live a thousand years, I never can forget it.

"The first thing that I distinctly saw was the shadow of a large cloud, which rolled slowly down the side of a huge mountain frowning over the height where I stood. The shadow moved down its steep, sunny side, threw a deep blackness over the sparkling river, and then passed off and climbed the opposite mountain on the other shore, leaving the world in the full blaze of noon. I could have stretched out my arms and shouted aloud—I could have fallen on my knees and worshipped—I could have committed any extravagance that ecstasy could suggest."

Unbounded joy, a total adoration of life and the state of being alive runs through this beautiful outpouring of Fanny's soul to her journal. It is like the writing of another person from the one who began the diary. What had changed her? What had transformed her into this thrilled, ecstatic young woman?

Fanny continued to act in New York for another fortnight,

while Pierce Butler came and went as much as he could, riding with her, or taking her on outings to Sandy Hook or to the Weehawken forest where years before Aaron Burr had shot Alexander Hamilton to death in a duel. "I am today twenty-three," she wrote on her birthday to Harriet. "Where is my life gone to? As the child said, 'Where does the light go when the candle is out?' "

On December 3 with the usual horrible early awakening Fanny left New York for Philadelphia. The day before, several friends had called to say goodbye and she felt touched by their warmth. It was even possible that she might miss New York, though returning to Philadelphia with its by now familiar buildings of pale marble seemed almost like a homecoming.

Two days later Fanny reappeared as Juliet and felt that she had given a bad performance. "How I do loathe the stage," she burst out to her diary afterward. "What a mass of wretched mumming mimicry it is." She described herself contemptuously as "an actress, a mimicker, a sham creature, me. . . ." Did her scorn for the falseness of acting rise from the fact that she had begun to feel the true emotion of love?

In Philadelphia she was now asked everywhere, appearing most often in the company of Pierce Butler. Within the closely knit circles of Philadelphia society there was much talk and shaking of heads over Pierce Butler's obvious infatuation for the actress. She had now more male admirers than ever to dance attendance upon her, but as one of them, Henry Wikoff, noted, Pierce Butler seemed the most likely to "carry off the splendid prize, and was envied and almost detested by a swarm of rivals."

There was much talk of slavery in the air and one day Fanny

was horrified to learn that to teach a slave to read or write was an offense punishable by a fine or imprisonment. The Negroes, she reported to her diary, "form the larger proportion of the population, by far [in the South]; and so great is the dread of insurrection on the part of the white inhabitants, that they are kept in the most brutish ignorance. . . ." Then with her prophetic gift she wrote these lines, which sound so fresh to us now: "Oh! what a breaking asunder of old manacles there will be, some of these fine days; what a fearful rising of the black flood; what a sweeping away, as by a torrent, of oppressions and tyrannies; what a fierce and horrible retaliation and revenge for wrong so long endured—so wickedly inflicted."

Despite the wearisomeness of her acting life Fanny seemed to grow more and more happy in Philadelphia, and her journal is radiant with lovely descriptions of the surrounding countryside where she went to ride or walk increasingly with Pierce Butler:

"The day was beautifully brilliant, clear and cold—winter, but winter in dazzling array of sunshine and crystal; blue skies, with light feathery strokes of white clouds running through them; dry, crisp, with the delicate rime tipping all the ruts with sparkling jewelry; and the waters fresh and bright and curling under the keen breath of the arrowlike wind."

Or:

"The river was frozen over, not, however, strongly enough to bear much, and every jutting rock was hung with pure glittering icicles that shone like jewels in the bright sunshine. Far down the river all was still and lonely and bright, yet wintry looking. The flow of the water and its splashing water were still; there was no breath of wind stirring the leafless boughs; the sunlight came down, warm and dazzling upon the silent, sparkling world, all clad in its shimmering ice robe. . . ."

By this time Fanny had come to know Pierce Butler's entire family including his brother, who was a cavalry officer, and his two sisters. One night she came home late, exhilarated after a party, and like any romantic young woman mooned before her bedroom window examining the sky. She had never before noticed that the stars had colors, "some reddish, some violet, and again others of the palest silver."

On the last day of the year Fanny set off on her travels again, this time farther south, first down the Delaware by boat, then across the northern tip of the state of Delaware on a railway that utilized one of her friend Mr. Stephenson's steam locomotives, then once again on a boat that steamed down the Elk River and across the Chesapeake Bay to Baltimore. The city seemed to her the newest looking she had seen yet and with its rambling stretches of red brick houses reminded her of England's "new" industrial cities, Birmingham or Manchester. It was New Year's Eve and she felt gloomy. Was Pierce Butler with her? We do not know. He accompanied her everywhere now, as much as he could —but perhaps his family had expected him to see the New Year in with them.

Two days later she was cheerful again. On her table she had a lovely nosegay of "roses, geraniums, rare heaths and perfect white camellias."

Exploring the city, Fanny and her father came upon a print

shop in the window of which were engravings of Mrs. Siddons as the Tragic Muse and John Philip Kemble playing Hamlet. For a long time Charles Kemble gazed at the wonderfully expressive faces of his brother and sister whom he would never see again. Fanny felt "a sort of sad surprise" at finding pictures of her aunt and uncle in an alien land where she and her father were strangers.

In Baltimore the Kembles played every night of the week to packed houses with their usual great success. Touring as they did without a troupe of their own, they were forced to rely on local supporting players, some of whose standards of acting were appalling. Fanny found that her Baltimore Romeo had gotten himself up in a costume so "puckered and beplaited and bepuffed" that he "looked like a magical figure growing out of a monstrous strange-colored melon." Their closing scene, when Juliet must take Romeo's dagger and stab herself, Fanny, with her wonderful sense of the ridiculous, could not resist describing verbatim in her journal. None of it is found in Shakespeare's play.

ROMEO: Rise, rise, my Juliet
And from this cave of death, this house of horror
Quick let me snatch thee to thy Romeo's arms.

"Here he pounced upon me, picked me up in his arms like an uncomfortable bundle and staggered down the stage with me."

JULIET (*aside*): Oh you've got me up horridly!—that'll never do, let me down, pray let me down.

ROMEO: There, breathe a vital spirit on thy lips,
And call thee back, my soul, to life and love.

JULIET (*aside*): Pray put me down; you'll certainly throw me down if you don't set me on the ground directly.

"In the midst of 'cruel, cursed fate' his dagger fell out of his dress; I, embracing him tenderly, crammed it back again, because I knew I should want it at the end."

ROMEO: Tear not our heart-strings thus!
They crack! they break! Juliet! Juliet! (*dies*)

JULIET (*to corpse*): Am I smothering you?
CORPSE (*to Juliet*): Not at all; could you be so kind, do you think, as to put my wig on again for me?—it has fallen off.
JULIET (*to corpse*): I'm afraid I can't, but I'll throw my muslin veil over it. You've broken the phial haven't you? (*Corpse nodded*)
JULIET (*to corpse*): Where's your dagger?
CORPSE (*to Juliet*): 'Pon my soul I don't know.

But somehow the show went on and pleased the audience.

On January 13 the little party set off for Washington over a road so terrible that one moment Fanny was thrown into her father's lap and the next half out the window. Here in the muddy, half-built capital of the country, Fanny made her debut before a distinguished audience in a tiny cube of a theater. Seated in one of the boxes was the venerable Dolly Madison, escorted by former President John Quincy Adams. Side by side in another of the boxes were Chief Justice of the Supreme Court, Judge Marshall, and one of his assistant Justices, Judge Story. In another part of the house, Senator Daniel Webster, the most distinguished orator of his day, was to be found.

"I have never seen any female acting at all comparable to hers," wrote Judge Story to his wife, adding that she had thrown the whole audience into tears. "The Chief Justice," he added, "shed them in common with younger eyes"—an interesting picture in American history of one of the country's most distinguished chief justices weeping in public.

Washington, a city planned but only partly built, struck Fanny "as a rambling, red brick image of futurity, where nothing *is,* but all things *are to be."* Nevertheless, she duly went sightseeing and visited the chambers of the Senate and the House of Representatives in the Capitol building, which in those days had no dome. She heard Daniel Webster speak "over a tremendous bustle and waving of feathers and rustling of silks" of other ladies who had also come to hear him orate. She saw the original Declaration of Independence and visited the War Office, where she viewed with curiosity various Indian relics—bows and arrows, canoes, smoking pipes, and pictures of some of the savage-looking chiefs. One day she was presented to President Andrew Jackson, whom she thought "a good specimen of a fine old well-battered soldier."

For relaxation, as was her usual custom, Fanny liked to go out riding. In addition to Pierce Butler, who followed her devotedly from city to city, there were always plenty of local admirers to offer their company and their horses as well—always of course under the chaperonage of the faithful Aunt Dall. Fanny usually hired a horse for herself, not wanting to take the responsibility of riding someone else's valuable animal. This she explained to a certain Mr. Fulton, relative of Robert Fulton, the inventor, who had offered to lend her one. So insistent was Mr. Fulton that she accept the loan of one of his horses that Fanny finally gave in, saying with a laugh that she ought to give him the usual two dollars hack fee just to feel right in her own mind.

Two days later Fanny came back from a round of calls in Washington to find her father looking very grave and troubled waiting for her in the company of another man. "Fanny," said Charles Kemble glancing at a letter in his hand, "something particularly disagreeable has occurred. Can you call to mind anything you said during the course of your Thursday's ride which was likely to be offensive to Mr. Fulton, or anything abusive of the country?"

Fanny, her dander beginning to rise at being asked about her own private affairs, coolly untied the strings of her bonnet and replied that she didn't remember one word of what she had said during the ride.

Charles Kemble's own eyes began to flash with anger. "Now, my dear, don't put yourself into a passion; compose yourself and recollect. Here is a letter I have just received." Mr. Kemble read aloud the letter, which declared that when Fanny had gone riding with Mr. Fulton, she had said that she usually preferred not to ride the horse of an American gentleman and had offered him two dollars for the hire of his. In addition she had spoken critically of America and its people. The story had spread all over Washington and had even reached Congress where there was a buzz of fury and resentment among some of its members. If, the letter continued, Mr. Kemble did not make some explanation or at least apology for his daughter's conduct, she would be hissed off the stage that evening.

It was one more example of America's extreme sensitivity—like the gawky adolescent that she was—to any kind of criticism from outsiders. It was said of Mrs. Frances Trollope, who had traveled all over the United States and then gone back to England and published in 1832 her none-too-favorable impressions of her visit, that she would be lynched or starved to death if she set foot in the country again.

Fanny's explanation of her entirely joking remark was simple and believable, and the delegate who had come to ask for the explanation took it away to spread about Washington. But would the city believe her? With her snobbish English accent and superior English ways did she not truly look down on all things American?

That evening Fanny went to the theater and got ready for the performance. Her side ached from tension and she had developed a nervous cough. Was an audience in the nation's capital capable of insulting a woman so grossly as to hiss her off the stage? In her anger at the incident she compared Washington to a tiny English village where gossip was spread by "half a dozen wives around their tea pots"—a description that is not unapt even today. Fortunately for Fanny the "half a dozen wives" did their work well, and when she made her entrance, applause, not hisses, greeted her. But it was embittering to realize that stories about her could become so easily twisted, and that it was possible for her supposedly adoring public to become disloyal.

Nor were the consequences of this slander at an end. Fanny returned to Philadelphia and on her first appearance received an immense ovation that lasted much longer than usual. Puzzled, she discovered during the next intermission that the story of her supposed attacks on America had been picked up by a Philadelphia newspaper. Someone (probably a jealous actor in the local company) had printed up a number of handbills repeating the accusations against her and distributed them around the theater, demanding that the audience demonstrate against poor Fanny. Charles Kemble went before the curtain to assure the audience that the story was of course false. There was more applause, but in fact he had not needed to make the speech. By giving Fanny a prolonged ovation at her first entrance, Philadelphia had proved its loyalty to her. "For my own part I love the whole city of Philadelphia from this time forth, for ever more," she wrote in her journal as she prepared to return to New York.

Fanny's arrival in that city coincided with a visit by the well-known authoress Catharine Maria Sedgwick. Miss Sedgwick, who was thought slightly eccentric for wearing her hair shoulder length instead of pinning it up according to the style of a more mature woman, which she was, came from a distinguished family that lived in the Berkshires—the beautiful range of hills found in western Massachusetts. Intelligent, critical, and very fond of the theater, she lost no time in going to see Fanny act. "She is a most captivating creature, steeped to the very lips in genius," was her reaction to Fanny's acting, which she wrote to her sister. "I have never seen any woman on the stage to be compared with her, nor ever an actor that delighted me so much. She is most effective in a true woman's character, fearful, tender, and true. On the stage she is beautiful, far more beautiful; her face is the mirror of her soul."

So fascinated was Miss Sedgwick by Fanny Kemble that the authoress took the trouble to call on her and found her to be "a quiet gentlewoman in her deportment." This meeting between the two gifted women resulted in their becoming fast friends, though Miss Sedgwick was twenty years older than Fanny. Miss Sedgwick had many relatives and friends in Boston including the clergyman Dr. William Ellery Channing, who had been raising his voice gently but insistently against the evil of slavery, and whose sermons Fanny had read with great enthusiasm. When Fanny came to Boston in the spring, as was planned, Miss Sedgwick promised to introduce Fanny to him, as well as to a whole circle of poets, writers, professors, and other intellectuals. The best minds in America were collected in Boston, she told Fanny, and Fanny could hardly wait to get there to challenge them and be challenged.

Meanwhile on one mild February day, Fanny and Pierce Butler took their horses aboard the ferry to Hoboken and there rode along the cliffs of the Hudson a hundred feet above the river. "We looked down its magnificent, broad, silvery avenue to the Narrows—the rocky gate that opens toward my home," she wrote in her journal. "New York lay bright and distinct on the opposite shore, glittering like a heap of toys in the sunny distance; the water toward Sandy Hook was studded with sails, and far up on the other side the river rolled away along shores that, even in this wintry time of bare trees and barren earth, looked gay and lovely in the sunshine." Pierce was neither particularly religious nor interested in the subject, but Fanny was. Gravely they discussed the different attitudes that men and women seemed to hold. Since women received so little education, Fanny pointed out, what else could they put their minds to but belief?

On April 13 the Kemble party, swelled now to four by the constant attendance of Mr. Butler, set off for Boston on a boat so huge and magnificent that it seemed like a "floating palace" to Fanny, who had never seen anything to compare with it in beauty and comfort. Next morning the steamer put in at Newport, Rhode Island, then sailed up the river to Providence, where Fanny and her party disembarked and got into an "extra"—a stagecoach all to themselves, which took them into Boston. The road was a paved turnpike and they made the forty-mile journey in the excellent time of six and a half hours.

Their hotel was the Tremont House, just opposite the theater where Charles and Fanny were to act. That evening Fanny put away her clothes after dinner, then settled down to write her diary, as was her custom, before going to bed. "Here we are in a new place!" she wrote. "How desolate and cheerless the constant changing of homes is." Then, curiously, she added: "The Scripture saith, 'There is no rest for the wicked'; and truly, I have never felt so convinced of my own wickedness as I have done since I have been in this country."

What did she mean?

CHAPTER 13

A Decision

TWO POWERFUL FORCES warred within Fanny Kemble's nature: passion and intellect. For an informally educated woman she had an unusually analytical mind: it examined all the issues of the day, political, moral, religious as well as those that pertained to everyday living. It probed, weighed, concluded. It was cool and objective and able to cut through to a conclusion.

But there was Fanny's other side, the one that had turned her into a remarkable actress in a single night. Intensity, willfulness, passion—it was this part of her character that had landed her in the frightening black of a cellar when she was a child, that caused her to respond with such excitement to storms, the rushing of water, the wind roaring in her ears as she galloped on a horse, unafraid, urging the animal on.

By the time Fanny reached Boston there could be no possible doubt that Pierce Butler was deeply in love with her, enough to break with the traditions of the narrow Philadelphia society in which he had grown up and to marry her. When and where he actually proposed Fanny does not tell us. Clearly, however, she took time in giving him an answer, while the two factions of her nature battled still harder.

Charming, good-looking, wealthy, Pierce Butler was one of the most eligible men in America. But after all there were Englishmen who possessed these assets to an even greater degree, and if Fanny returned to England she could undoubtedly have her pick of them. Married to Pierce Butler, she would have to live among men and women with whom she had little in common—the dull conservative society of Philadelphia, where the people were not particularly interested in the arts, or literature, or any of the things that Fanny's mind and soul fed on. Once married, as she had observed, American women didn't go out much. They retired to the walls of the ballroom or from parties altogether. Once married, a woman totally gave up any right to independence. By law, her property became her husband's. Her children, when she bore them, belonged to him also. A wife, in fact, was her husband's property—his chattel. If Fanny married Pierce Butler he would expect her to retire from the stage and become completely dependent on him, she, who entirely on her own had earned thousands of dollars by her acting. Not that she would lack money as Mrs. Pierce Butler: Pierce seemed already to be extremely well off, with the expectation of inheriting more wealth, though what its source was she still did not know. Something to do with farms—plantations, Pierce had once vaguely explained.

And what of his actual character? He was very young, one year her junior, indolent enough to pursue her wherever she traveled, spoiled and stubborn enough to insist on having his way by making her his wife.

Reason then warned against the marriage. But what of passion?

The next day after arriving in Boston she rode out with Pierce to visit Cambridge, seat of Harvard University, and beyond it to the Mount Auburn cemetery, a tract of a hundred acres of lovely hills and ravines. Avenues named for the various trees—Linden Walk or Beech Walk—had been cut through it, and occasionally they came upon a gravestone glimmering palely in the woods. Fanny thought it very lovely. Soon she would return there, not on a day's outing of pleasure, but from sad necessity.

That evening Charles Kemble made his Boston debut as Hamlet, a part that his daughter always thought he played very beautifully. " 'Tis curious that when I see him act I have none of the absolute feeling of contempt for the profession that I have while acting myself. What he does appears indeed like the work of an artist; and though I always lament that he loves it as he does, and has devoted so much care and labor to it as he has, yet I certainly respect acting more while I am seeing him act than at any other time."

The next night Fanny made her own Boston debut receiving the by now predictable acclaim that she drew wherever she performed. The next morning she looked out of her hotel room window, from which she could see the box office of the Tremont Theater. A crowd had collected in front and when the doors were opened in surged the mob, shouting and pummeling one another.

She was surprised to see various coarse-looking men among them, not the ordinary kind of theatergoer at all. Later she learned that they were speculators who bought up boxes at regular prices and resold them at a high profit to people desperate to see the celebrated Miss Kemble. Some of these men smeared their clothes with molasses and sugar, which kept the more respectable people in the crowd, not wanting their own clothes to be stained, back from the box office. "This is ingenious and deserves a reward," commented the practical Fanny to her journal.

Fanny immediately felt at home in Boston. The houses looked like English houses; the Common reminded her of London parks, and even the streets of the two cities seemed alike. Miss Sedgwick proved to be right about the intellectual climate of Boston. Here were people with discriminating minds and tastes. Fanny met Miss Sedgwick again and as promised was introduced to Dr. William Ellery Channing, whose prose she so much admired. Fanny wanted to talk to him about the cause she now deeply believed in—abolishing slavery—but Dr. Channing wished to discuss the theater with her. Dr. Channing won, much to Fanny's disappointment.

If Fanny took to Boston, the reverse was also true. Harvard students and faculty mobbed her performances. The poorer students would even pawn their books or clothing for the price of a ticket to see her act. Young people gathered outside the Tremont House at the hour she usually went riding just to catch a glimpse of her, and every young Boston girl wore her hair in "Fanny Kemble curls," imitating the fascinating actress's hair style.

Spring came on. Fanny and Pierce took their horses on the

ferry across the mouth of the Charles River and rode north up the shore to Chelsea Beach near the town of Lynn. As always the sight of the sea aroused and excited Fanny's spirits. Even though it was only April the day was hot, and she and Pierce were able to wander along the edge of the water collecting, in that absorbed way of the beachcomber, mussel shells, quartz, little stones, and pieces of seaweed. "The thin, thin rippling waves came like silver leaves spreading themselves over the glittering sand with just a little sparkling, pearly edge, like the cream of a bright glass of champagne." They came to a hut from which hunters shot plover, and lay under the warm sun side by side on the roof of it, intimate, absorbed in one another's company. Another day she rode out to the Blue Hills with Pierce, and finding them strange and frighteningly lonely she was glad that she was not there without him.

More and more she became drawn to this man who was gently, perseveringly breaking down the reserves of the woman whom he wanted more than anything else in the world.

Talk about the pair multiplied. Was there an engagement? None had been announced but there were all sorts of rumors. The idea of marriage between the two frankly troubled Miss Sedgwick. Writing to a friend she described Fanny as "a complex being, made up of glorious faculties, delightful accomplishments, immeasurable sensibilities—and half a hundred faults." While acknowledging Pierce Butler to be "a gentlemanly man, with good sense and an amiable disposition," Miss Sedgwick warned that he was "so infinitely inferior to her that the experiment of marriage might be dangerous."

Fanny finished her Boston engagement and returned to New York where Philip Hone, her great admirer, again went to see her perform. She played "with the most affecting pathos," he reported to his diary, adding ruefully that it was "probably her last engagement if the report be true that she is married or about to marry Mr. Pierce Butler of Philadelphia."

That June as the heat came on Mr. Kemble decided to combine the business of acting with a holiday. He and Fanny would go north to Albany and then on to some of the Canadian cities such as Quebec and Montreal. But their trip would be leisurely and they would take time to see some of the great natural wonders such as Niagara Falls. Pierce, naturally, would come with them. Mr. Kemble also asked an odd, piratical-looking Englishman whom he had met in New York named Edward Trelawny, who was an explorer and writer and who had been a close friend of Byron during the poet's last days in Greece. Fanny was amazed by his appearance. His face was "as dark as a moor's with a wild, strange look about the eye and forehead and a mark like a scar upon his cheek." Exceptionally large, he had a way of walking "as if he didn't know where he was going and didn't much wish to go anywhere." On his browned hands he wore two curious rings, one made of elephant's hair. His whole appearance gave her "an idea of toil, hardship, peril, and adventure." Fanny was fascinated by his company and his many stories of Byron, whose writings she had always adored.

The party journeyed by boat to Albany, where Fanny and her father acted for one night with their usual success. A jouncing coach took them to Schenectady, where they were then able to travel on the wonderful new Mohawk Canal to Utica. Fanny enjoyed the placid motion of the canal boat, which moved along at a speed of four and a half miles an hour. The little group sat out on deck while Mr. Trelawny read *Don Quixote* to them, but found it a nuisance when the boatman shouted "Low Bridge!" about every fifteen minutes and they all had to flatten themselves to avoid concussion.

Fifteen miles north of Utica were the Trenton Falls, a sight not to be missed. Early on the morning of July 12 the little party set out from Utica to view them, Fanny and Pierce seated side by side opposite her father and aunt inside the coach, the huge figure of Mr. Trelawny looming up from the box on top of it. It was a bright, breezy day. Summer was at its height. The ripening grain, the sloping fields, the silvery fences all gave pleasure to Fanny's enchanted eyes.

A guide who ran an inn close to the falls led them through a wood to the brink of a boiling river into which the water fell. Then single file the group started up a narrow path made slippery and treacherous by the blowing spray of the falls. The guide told of a young girl who had recently missed her footing and drowned in the foaming water of the river below. Fanny was overcome with a terror that she had never felt before. Walking in front of her Pierce Butler kept calling out encouragement to her in a kindly, reassuring tone.

They reached the first fall, which burst out of the side of the mountain "like a great rolling heap of amber." Mr. Kemble, Aunt Dall, and the guide went on directly, but Fanny and Pierce loitered behind, "flinging light branches and flowers upon the blood-colored torrent that whirled and dragged and tossed them down to the plunge beneath." Mr. Trelawny, ignoring the pair, flung himself down under a roof of rock by the rushing water. Fanny and Pierce went on—alone.

The next fall was circular in shape with an arching rainbow rising from its depths. The pair crawled down to a narrow ridge and sat with their feet dangling over the black, thundering mass of water. Fanny grew dizzy with the sound and the sight and cautiously the two moved on. All her senses had begun to reel with the rushing of the water and its hypnotic spell of danger. They came to another fall, and Pierce was lifting Fanny up onto a fallen tree trunk when Mr. Trelawny came by. He stopped and spoke to them for a moment, then tactfully moved on. Again they were alone, talking and dipping their hands into the fresh water.

Was this the moment that Fanny joyfully, trustingly yielded her heart to Pierce Butler and agreed to marry him? Her journal does not say, but then it was carefully edited for publication and anything so intimate would have been omitted in the interests of good taste. And yet what is left in, the careful description of Pierce Butler and herself *alone,* seems to indicate that this was the moment she accepted her future husband.

The afternoon wore away and the group reassembled to start the journey back. Fanny, like a dutiful wife, followed behind Pierce along the slimy, treacherous path by the river with the roar of the falls filling her ears. Mr. Trelawny assured her that the cataract at Niagara, which he had seen, would take away all memory of this one.

But Fanny must have known that nothing could take away the memory of that afternoon.

CHAPTER 14

Pierce Butler's Secret

FOUR DAYS LATER Fanny opened her eyes and saw Aunt Dall with blood all over her face from a gash on her forehead. Fanny herself was lying pinned beneath the bulk of her father. They had left Rochester very early in the morning intending to eat breakfast at an inn in the town of Murray. The stagecoach had only one door, and in order for the passengers to alight directly on the doorstep of the hostelry the driver had swung the clumsy vehicle around in an abrupt circle, and the carriage, slung very high, American style, had overturned.

"I'm not hurt! I'm not hurt!" Fanny shouted despite the weight of her father pressing upon her. When he was helped up she was able to get to her feet in time to see two men carrying Mr. Trelawny into the inn where they laid him on a bed in an upstairs room. Aunt Dall was led to another looking very white and shaken. To Fanny's great relief Mr. Trelawny began to stir and coming to, assured her that he was not hurt. An experienced traveler, he got up and began to bandage poor Dall's wound. Fanny's father had hurt his leg slightly but Pierce—thank God!—was totally unhurt. On the whole the party considered themselves lucky to have escaped—so they thought—with such minor injuries. In Fanny's opinion of her travels in America, it was miraculous that "anybody in this country ever arrives at the end of a land journey at all."

Having breakfasted, the travelers pushed on, eager to reach what would be, they hoped, the highlight of their trip—Niagara Falls. As they crossed into Canada Fanny became more and more nervous with expectation. The only conveyance available to take them to the Falls was a simple cart, into which they climbed eagerly. Three miles outside the village of Niagara the driver stopped the wagon for a moment and they heard for the first time the distant rumble of the falling water, while rising over the woods by the Niagara River they could see a cloud of silver spray rising slowly into the sky.

Fanny became frenzied with impatience. When the wagon finally arrived at Niagara House, through which, in those days, visitors gained entrance to the Falls, she jumped down and, not waiting for anyone else, rushed through the building and down a steep footpath cut in the rocks. Through a thicket of trees she could just make out the white foam of the Falls up ahead. Faster and faster she ran while behind her the excited voice of Mr. Trelawny, who had seen the Falls before, called out, "Go on. Go on. Don't stop!" In another moment she had reached Table Rock just as Trelawny caught up with her, and seizing her by the arm dragged her to the brink of the thundering Falls.

"I could not speak," she wrote to Harriet, "and I could hardly breathe; I felt as if I had an iron band across my breast. I watched the green, glassy heaps go plunging down, down, down; each mountainous mass of water, as it reached the dreadful brink, recoiling, as in horror, from the abyss; . . . The mysterious chasm with its uproar of voices seemed like the watery mouth of hell. I looked and listened till the wild excitement of the scene took such possession of me that, but for the strong arm that held me back, I really think I should have let myself slide down into the gulf. It was long before I could utter, and as I began to draw my breath I could only gasp out, 'O God! O God!' No words can describe either the scene itself, or its effect upon me."

The party spent three days at Niagara, most of which Fanny in an almost hypnotized state spent "by the water, under the water, on the water and more than half in the water." She lay on the rocks by the very edge of the foaming bowl into which the water crashes down with a thunderous roar. She walked under the huge stone arch that creates the waterfall. Drenched, blown by gusts of wind created by the tremendous drop of the water, she could hardly bear to tear herself away.

A few miles down the river from the Falls is the famous whirlpool where the strangely colored water—"like discolored turquoise," Fanny described it—churns around in a "sullen, savage, dark basin." It turned Fanny's mind to thoughts of evil and death. "Drowning in that deep, dark, wicked-looking whirlpool," she wrote her friend, "would be hideous compared to being dashed to death amid the dazzling spray of Niagara."

From Niagara Falls the party went by boat across Lake Ontario, and entering the St. Lawrence River passed through the lovely area of the Thousand Islands on their way down to Montreal and after that Quebec. The idyllic summer wore away and autumn found Fanny acting once more in New York. To friends at home she now announced the news that she was engaged to be married. "I shall not return to England, not even to visit it now, certainly never to make my home there again. . . . My feeling about the stage you know full well and will rejoice with me that there is a prospect of my leaving it."

Before marrying and retiring from the theater Fanny felt it her duty to act one more full season for her father. The money that she earned she would then make over to him, and he with Aunt Dall could return to England with the family fortune mended. But fate now intervened for poor Aunt Dall. Unaware of the fact at the time the carriage had overturned, she had been injured internally by the accident. In the spring of 1834 Aunt Dall became seriously ill. The doctors told Fanny that her aunt could never fully recover but would be an invalid for the rest of her life. Aunt Dall had no money of her own, and when Fanny retired from the stage, as she planned to that coming June, neither would she.

Frantically Fanny cast about for some way to give financial independence to her dear aunt who had devotedly helped to raise her, who had been at her side through the many trials of her stage career, and who had made the sacrifice of coming to America and taking on all the hardships of a traveling actor's life. Suddenly an idea flashed through Fanny's mind. The Philadelphia publisher, Mr. Carey! Mr. Carey had offered her a very large sum of money to print her impressions of America. This money Fanny could give to Aunt Dall.

Fanny signed a contract with the delighted publisher. But her generous, impulsive gesture proved to be in vain. On the twenty-fourth of April Aunt Dall died in Fanny's arms. It was the first death of someone really close to her that she had ever known, and Fanny was heartbroken. Fanny took her aunt for burial to a lonely lovely place in Mount Auburn Cemetery where Pierce and she used to sit together the previous spring. "I wished her to lie there," Fanny wrote to Harriet, "for life and love and youth and death have their trysting place at the grave."

On June 7, 1834, Fanny and Pierce were married at Christ Church in Philadelphia. The wedding, as provided by the wealthy Butler family, was a lavish one, and all society turned out to see the radiant bride in her sumptuous white dress and the equally radiant bridegroom. Two weeks later Fanny made her farewell from the stage. That night, it is said, Pierce himself played the flute in the orchestra, and when Fanny was taking her curtain calls he rushed out of the pit and embraced her—the wife whom he had finally captured.

With Fanny Kemble's retirement, America lost "the most intellectual, passionate, and original English actress of the age," wrote Joseph N. Ireland in his *Records of the New York Stage*. "To the state and dignity of the Kemble school she added the fire and impetuosity of her own genius; from her mother she inherited a grace and fascination in her comic delineations that no other of the blood of Kemble ever knew. . . . Her triumph in America was complete; she was the acknowledged Queen of Tragedy from Boston to New Orleans, without a rival near her throne."

So far in her short life Fanny had only played at tragedy. Now she was about to partake of it. Soon after she was married, as the wife of Pierce Butler and therefore completely dependent on him, Fanny learned for the first time that the entire money on which she now lived came from plantations in the Sea Islands of Georgia. Pierce Butler, her husband, the man she loved and whom she had promised to honor and obey, was that most despicable of men—a *slave owner.*

Part Two

There never was a war that was
not inward.

—Marianne Moore

CHAPTER 15

Fanny's First Journal

"WHAT CAN I TELL you of myself? My life and all its occupations are of a sober neutral tint. I am busy preparing my Journal for the press. I read but little and that of the old fashioned kind. I have never read much and am disgracefully ignorant. I am looking forward with delight to hours of quiet study, and the mental hoards in store for me. I am busy preparing to leave town; I am at present, and have been ever since my marriage staying in the house of my brother-in-law, and feel not a little anxious to be in a home of my own. . . .

"I please myself much in the fancying of furniture and fitting up of the house; and I look forward to a garden, greenhouse, and dairy among my future interests. . . .

"My pets are a horse, a bird, and a black squirrel and I do not see exactly what more a reasonable woman could desire. Human companionship, indeed, at present I do not have much of

. . . you can form no idea—none—none—of the intellectual dearth and drought in which I am existing at present."

Vapors of boredom rise from these lines that Fanny sent to a friend in England describing her married life. In one day the exhilaration of acting, the stimulus of new persons and places, the feeling of always being the center of attention had been cut out of her life, and she now lived among staid, quiet people who could only be described as dull. She had longed to leave the stage, to take up a calm, orderly, above all respectable existence—or so she thought. This kind of life based entirely on her attractive husband, whom she adored, Fanny had believed would be enough. And yet what was to channel off all her formidable energy working always hand in hand with that intent, ever-inquiring mind? How could it be harnessed in some way?

For six months after her marriage Fanny was forced to live with her new in-laws while her future home just outside of Philadelphia was renovated and redecorated. What must these stuffy, conventional people have thought of such a head-strong woman, scarcely much older than a girl, who spoke her views so plainly and seemed, in her haughty English way, vaguely patronizing of them? Time and again she mentioned the names of friends among the British nobility and spoke of being received in the houses of people with the highest connections. How could this be, they wondered in their snobbish way, when after all she was nothing but an *actress?*

Even more extraordinary was Fanny's behavior toward Pierce. Like all women of her time now that she was married she was expected to submit entirely to her husband's will. For a wife to express opinions differing sharply from her husband's was unheard of. Yet almost from the day of the wedding, Fanny had repeatedly denounced slavery and upheld the cause of the abolitionists, even though she now knew that owning slaves was her husband's livelihood.

Then there was the matter of her journal. Since Fanny had signed a legal contract with the Philadelphia publisher Mr. Carey, he was planning to go ahead and print. Pierce thought her book insulting to America in general and his circle of friends in particular. He pleaded with Fanny to break the contract, but determined not to be ruled by her husband's will—no one, after all, had *ever* ruled her—she refused, saying that the journal was an honest and not at all unflattering record of her impressions of the new country. Angry, Pierce went to Mr. Carey and offered him ten thousand dollars not to print the book, but the clever publisher turned him down, realizing that the journal would create a sensation and earn a much larger sum. Pierce then appointed himself editor of the journal and began to cut out large sections of Fanny's carefully written prose. No one had ever dictated to her before about what or how she wrote and indignant, she would not allow her husband to now.

She had tacked on to the end of the journal a long tirade against slavery and this angered Pierce Butler most of all. How could his own wife, who owed him the deepest respect and allegiance, want to publish views that were directly contrary to his own? To Fanny's rage, Pierce Butler destroyed the section altogether. Did she not realize, he demanded, that Philadelphia was close to the South and the majority of its people were sympathetic to slavery? If her antislavery chapter were printed, the people might easily tear down the Butlers' house and burn its furniture, "a favorite mode of remonstrance in these parts with those who advocate the rights of the unhappy blacks," as Fanny wrote sourly to Harriet St. Leger.

More and more angered by his criticisms Fanny, typically for a bride of few months, thought of running away. No one had ever treated her so coldly, so ungently before. Pierce had known what she was like before they were married—why did he expect her to change? What she had not known before she had accepted him was that he owned hundreds and hundreds of slaves whose unpaid work bought every stick of furniture for their new house, every piece of clothing that she now wore. The bitterness of this thought was too much; how could she stay another moment with such a man? Yet how could she leave her handsome husband on whom not only her life but her heart depended? Once again passion intervened before there could be any break in the marriage and bound her more closely to Pierce than ever. That fall Fanny found that she was going to have a child.

In December she finally managed to move to her new home called—far more grandly than it merited—Butler Place. A simple white house fronted with two tiers of verandas, it was located in Branchtown on the New York–Philadelphia turnpike, too near for Fanny's tastes to the much-traveled road from which clouds of dust were constantly kicked up. Fanny busied herself with making the house as attractive as possible, though the rooms were disappointingly small and without architectural merit. She was fond of various shades of blue and violet, and there was always a smell of Russian leather in the places where she lived. As warmer weather came on she began to plan a flower garden and the planting of an avenue of trees that would give some character to Butler Place. It surprised her how few people cultivated flowers in America—only the essential fruit and vegetables. To Fanny, flowers were an essential too.

She formed schemes of mixing into community life and doing good as any gentlewoman of her time would have done in an equivalent English village. One idea, teaching the children of her gardener and tenant farmer to read and write, was greeted with contemptuous amazement. Wasn't there a village school in Branchtown, as the law required there be in every American community? Why should her neighbors be beholden to the "lady of the manor" for their children's education? That was not the American way.

Again a woman of her position would have gone visiting among the poor of an English village, bringing gifts of clothing, food, and medicines. But in America Fanny soon discovered there were no poor of the desperate, wretched kind that existed in England—people less well off, certainly, but none so lacking in pride as to welcome someone's personal charity.

As the lady of the manor and English in addition, she thought it might be a graceful gesture to hold a fete for the villagers on the Fourth of July, a big dinner out under the trees with wine and beer for all. No one told her that all the guests were Quakers and not only did not drink but also disapproved of the habit. Fanny's holiday party passed off in an embarrassment of glum silence.

Meanwhile, Pierce Butler could not prevent publication of his wife's journal without bringing a law suit onto himself, for having married Fanny, her book, her contract, and all that she owned had become his property. The journal appeared early in 1835 and, as Mr. Carey rightly predicted, stirred up a tremendous uproar. True she had left all the names blank, but people she had met and mentioned in the journal could easily recognize the occasion she was referring to and identify themselves. "Mr. —— came in to bid us goodbye. . . . He is a nice, good-tempered Irishman with more tongue than brains." How, one wonders, did Mr. —— react to this tart description of himself? "On the stairs met the odious Dr. —— who came into the drawing room without asking or being asked. . . . I should have liked to throw my tea at him!" What must the worthy Dr. —— have thought of Fanny's scornful opinion of him?

One who read her book and reacted to it with a kind of bemused indignation was the kindly Mr. Hone, whose dinner party in honor of Fanny he found described in none-too-flattering terms. Fortunately she had given a glowing picture of the beauty of his daughter and this allowed him to excuse "many of her impertinences." Others, however, felt no such mildness toward her. Among the impartial people everyone agreed that the journal was a fascinating record of the time, that many of her criticisms of America were just, and that she was a perceptive and brilliant reporter.

On May 27, 1835, Fanny gave birth to a baby girl, Sarah, or Sally as she was always called. Most women accepted the pain of childbirth as their lot. Not Fanny. "I cannot believe that women were intended to suffer as much as they do, and be as helpless as they are," she wrote to Harriet, adding quite correctly that undoubtedly the wearing of tight corsets and other restrictive garments undermined the health of the women of her day. She had wished for a boy. The lot of a man seemed infinitely preferable to that of the kept-down woman, deprived of her many natural rights including extensive education. But the baby was a great comfort to her: now at least she had something to which she could direct her energies. Her days had meaning again and her life a purpose, something that her marriage seemed somehow to have taken away.

She continued to brood over the problem of slavery. One day Pierce told her that the cotton lands of his Georgia plantation were becoming exhausted since the crop was never rotated. Slightly sarcastically, he asked her how she would like to go with him and his slaves to richer lands in Mississippi where a fortune was to be made. Fanny's joyful and earnest reply was that she would go with delight if they could place their slaves on "a more humane and Christian footing."

"I cannot tell you what joy it would fill me, if we could only do this," she rhapsodized to Harriet, pouring forth her dreams of going among the slaves and teaching them by her "personal example," and explaining to them her "principles" and "purpose" even if she was not allowed to teach them to read and write. Most of these ideas were of course farfetched and full of idealistic wishful thinking.

In her fervent desire to help their slaves she had repeatedly asked if she could come with Pierce when he found it necessary to go down to the plantations, but he would not hear of the idea, pointing out that the swampy country was rife with malaria except during winter, and that she would be risking the life of the baby. Even Harriet St. Leger was shocked at Fanny's eagerness to take her infant and herself to this dangerous, scarcely civilized part of the country and expressed herself on the subject. Fanny replied indignantly, "I never contemplated sacrificing my child's, or anybody else's health to my desire for 'doing good.' . . . But you must remember that *we are slave owners* and live by slave labor. . . . If the question of slavery does not concern us, in God's name whom does it concern?"

Like the more vehement abolitionists of the day Fanny had come to look upon slavery as a sinful practice against God. Now she became determined to cast out that sin from, of all people, her husband. "We are possessed of power and opportunity to do a great work," she wrote in a later letter to Harriet. By freeing his slaves Mr. Butler could set an example to the other slave owners. "How can I bear to think that this great occasion for doing good or dealing justly may be neglected or wasted by us. . . . Oh how I wish I was a man!" she cried out to Harriet. "How I wish I owned these slaves, instead of being supported (disgracefully, as it seems to me) by their unpaid labor."

So the issue of slavery lay like a sharp glittering sword between husband and wife, who at the same time were deeply in love with one another.

That summer Fanny went for the first time to Stockbridge, in the Berkshire Hills of western Massachusetts, to visit her friends the Sedgwicks, whose antislavery views she found so sympathetic. The beauty of the country, its lakes, valleys, and woods immediately cast a spell over her that would repeatedly draw her back to the region for the rest of her life.

A winter and another summer passed, each day much alike for Fanny in her solitary existence with her baby. In the fall of 1836 Pierce Butler learned that he would have to spend the winter with his brother on one of the plantations they owned jointly in the Georgia Sea Islands below Savannah. Fanny longed to go with him, but there was no place even nearby suitable to take a baby. Instead another plan was made for her winter. Since she would be alone, Pierce suggested, why did she not take the baby and nurse and spend the winter in England with her family, whom naturally she had missed greatly? Pierce would then join her in the spring and meet her relations and all the grand and interesting people she had often spoken of. Fanny could show him her beloved England—a land where slavery did not exist.

At the beginning of November Fanny, Sally, and nurse Margery O'Brien took ship from New York to Liverpool. She was going home.

CHAPTER 16

England Again

CALM SEAS had attended Fanny's first voyage to America. The return was altogether different. A four-day gale struck the little packet boat, and the window of her cabin had to be boarded up against the violence of the waves. Suffocating, she pleaded with the steward to open it up again, which he did, and water came crashing into the cabin sweeping everything before it. With the window boarded over again, Fanny, her baby, and the nurse lay in the dark, airless compartment while the groaning ship shuddered and heaved under the assault of the thrashing seas. At the height of the storm the vessel sprang its mainmast and tossed about so violently that Fanny was certain they were lost. Nurse Margery O'Brien sank to her knees and prayed the night through while Fanny beheld a sudden vision of her whole life in review, as people are said to do just before they think they are going to die. To keep up her courage as the foundering ship lurched on she sang to herself every song she could think of and in this manner weathered the storm.

"I find London more beautiful, more rich, more royal than ever," was her reaction on seeing the great city again where once she had been a star. A joyful reunion took place with her family: Charles Kemble, looking much older and preparing to retire from the stage; Mrs. Kemble with her round, merry eyes, also more fragile in appearance; and Fanny's older brother, John, who had become a literary scholar and who had brought back a bride from Germany where he had attended a university. Then there was her handsome younger brother, Henry, a dashing army officer, and "baby" Adelaide, not quite twenty-three, who had developed her voice sufficiently to be planning a career in opera.

There were also countless friends to see. In total contrast to her solitary, unsocial life of the two previous years, she went everywhere to parties, balls, and receptions. A few weeks after her arrival Charles Kemble made his farewell appearance on the stage, and Fanny feared for him in his retirement. Like his sister Mrs. Siddons, acting had become a drug for him. How could he live without his nightly dose of applause? Fanny was thankful that she had given up acting before the excitement of it had become necessary for her.

Spring came on. Fanny looked forward eagerly to the arrival of Pierce. Unfortunately he was a delegate to a convention being held at Harrisburg, Pennsylvania, to rewrite the state's constitution. Originally scheduled for February the meeting had been pushed back to May. Fanny was impatient for her husband to come, eager to show the attractive man she had married to her family and friends. She missed him. She loved him. . . .

That spring the old king, William the Fourth, died and a tiny slip of a girl, not yet nineteen, ascended the throne of England at a time when the country was just bursting into the bloom of all its industrial might. Fanny, through the offices of a highly connected friend, was present when Queen Victoria addressed Parliament for the first time. Fanny thought her voice exquisite and had never heard words spoken more musically than when the Queen took breath and said: "My Lords and Gentlemen . . ."

In midsummer the Harrisburg Convention finally adjourned, but temporarily, agreeing to meet the following October. This gave Pierce Butler only a short time in England before he would have to return to America. Excitedly, Fanny and Sally went to Liverpool to meet his boat. But the sea proved treacherous again. The boat was two weeks late, plagued by unfavorable storms and winds, while Fanny waited impatiently at a little beach resort just north of Liverpool where, unlike that in the foul city, the air was fresh and clean.

When Pierce finally arrived the reunion was a joyful one. One sight of him was enough to make her heart start up, to make her realize, despite their differences, how much she loved him. For two crowded weeks she introduced him to her family, her friends, and England itself. As only Pierce could be, he was charming to all whom he met. England's aristocratic system pleased him; he felt at home with it and was pleased by Fanny's many titled friends. As for Fanny, what more graceful compliment could he have paid her than to come all that distance, traveling in slow, uncomfortable, even dangerous style to fetch home his beloved wife?

They returned to Liverpool and boarded a ship that was packed with emigrants to America. Again the wind betrayed, and the next day they awoke to find the ship had been unable to sail and could not go for another twenty-four hours. That night the Butlers were able to see William Macready, now England's leading actor of the day, in a performance of *Macbeth*. What Fanny could not have remotely foreseen was that one day, through strange twists and turns of fate, she would find herself acting opposite him in the very same play.

The voyage back to New York took thirty-seven storm-ridden days. Fanny was sick the entire time (actually she was in the very early stages of her second pregnancy), and when she emerged from her cabin in New York she looked ghostlike and could hardly walk from weakness. The Butlers put up at a New York hotel while she recovered her strength. Pierce then went on to Harrisburg and when Fanny felt well enough she followed him. There was a railway now across Pennsylvania, but it stopped just short of the capital itself and Fanny had to carry little Sally for over a quarter of a mile in the intense cold. As a result the child developed a worrying cough, but aside from that Fanny, as she always did anything new, enjoyed her experience among the rough delegates who were fashioning the new constitution. She found no intellectual companionship among these men, who liked to call on the famous actress and take her riding across the purple highlands of the Susquehanna Valley. Nonetheless, as she commented to Harriet St. Leger, "the shrewdness, the sound sense, the original observations and the experience of some of these men are striking and remarkable. Though not one of them can speak grammatically, they all speak fluently, boldly, easily, without effort or hesitation."

Returning to Butler Place, Fanny once again had time to muse on the basic problem that to a certain extent besets all marriages: "In the relationship of friendship there is perfect agreement . . . to be neither dependent on, nor controlled by, each other's will. In the relation of marriage," she realized, "this is impossible. A woman should, I think, love her husband better than anything on earth except her own soul; which, I think, a man should respect above everything on earth but his own soul." There it was in a nutshell: how could Fanny love Pierce Butler "better than anything on earth," and, despising slavery, love her own soul as well? As she philosophized to Harriet, who had never married: "It is indeed a pretty difficult problem and perhaps you have chosen, if not the wiser and better, at any rate the easier and safer part."

That winter word came from home that Adelaide was going on the stage as a professional singer. Fanny's reaction was rather characteristic of an older sister—vague disapproval mixed with the anxiety of one already experienced in the theater. "I hope she may succeed to the full extent of her desires for I do not think hers is a nature that would be benefited by the bitter medicine of disappointment. . . . Natural talent is sufficient for a certain degree of success in acting but not in singing . . . the tone of the voice itself being often fatally affected by the loss of self-possession." Nor did Fanny approve of her father's choice of Paris for

Adelaide's debut, pointing out that two celebrated prima donnas of their day had both failed on their first appearance in the French city.

Fanny's life continued to wind on in the dull, conventional routine of a young wife and mother living in a suburb of a large city, her existence always beclouded by the thought of slavery and the fact that all she owned, the very food she put into her mouth was gotten by the labor of unpaid, subjugated human beings. Fanny had always prided herself on being systematic, but felt she had outdone herself when on the exact same day in May as Sally had been born two years before and almost at the same hour, she gave birth to another girl named Frances Kemble Butler. Now there were two Fannys.

When the summer heat came on the Butlers went north to stay at Rockaway Beach outside of New York City in a big, rambling hotel near the ocean. As always, Fanny loved being by the sea, but the lack of private changing rooms she found positively shocking. All the women and young children undressed before one another in the single room of a bathing hut; and the men in another. It was not to be believed!

At a ball in the Rockaway Hotel Fanny chanced to see the courteous Mr. Hone again. He had long since forgiven her for "her inconsiderate girlish remarks" in her journal and immediately went up to her and asked her to dance. Fanny, deeply moved by his attentions, thanked him with great earnestness. Tears even came into her eyes for a moment. Mr. Hone wrote in his journal of this meeting, "The tear which stood in her flashing eyes convinced me that this highly gifted woman possesses that warmth of heart for which I have never failed to give her credit."

From Rockaway the Butlers stopped temporarily in the dreadful heat of New York while Pierce took treatments for a rheumatic complaint, before taking the boat up the river to Hudson, New York, from where a stagecoach brought them to Lenox, another town in the Berkshire Hills. Here now lived Charles Sedgwick, brother of Catharine Maria, and his beautiful wife Elizabeth, who were keeping a school in their own house. Fanny was delighted to have the stimulating company of the Sedgwicks, though unfortunately with Pierce present the absorbing subject of abolition could not be discussed. As always, the beauty of the country charmed Fanny's eyes.

"Immediately sloping before me, the green hillside, on the summit of which stands the house I am inhabiting, sinks softly down to a small valley, filled with thick, rich woods in the center of which a little jewel-like lake lies gleaming. Beyond this valley the hills rise one above another to the horizon, where they scoop the sky with a broken, irregular outline that the eye dwells on with ever new delight as its colors flow and vary with the ascending or descending sunlight, and all the shadowy procession of the clouds."

Here in this lovely environment among sympathetic people, the sad news reached Fanny of her mother's death. A line of writing on a piece of paper made it seem scarcely real. Mrs. Kemble had been a lively, interesting woman, courageous in adversity, with high critical standards and a great sense of fun. All these qualities she had passed on to her daughter.

And then occurred a most unexpected turn to Fanny's life that helped distract her mind from the death of her mother. Pierce Butler found it essential to go again to his Georgia plantations, probably for a period of three or four months. The previous winter he had had the company of his brother, but this year John Butler was ill and could not go. Now all of a sudden, Pierce illogically reversed all his reasons for not taking Fanny when she had pleaded with him to go south and said she might come. Life in a small, crudely furnished house in the middle of rice swamps, Pierce warned, would scarcely be comfortable. There would be no flour (cornmeal was used to make bread) and no fresh meat except for game. He would send down barrels of various provisions including salt pork, but their diet would be monotonous. They would live on an island and the only other white person on it living with them would be the overseer of the slaves. The nearest town was a small one and the society crude.

But Fanny was wild to go. "I set my face toward a part of the country where the whole manner of existence is repugnant to my feelings," she wrote to Harriet. Now at last she was doing her duty. Now at last she had the opportunity to serve the great and righteous cause in which she believed so ardently. She would open Pierce's eyes to the evil of slavery and make him free his bondsmen, and his action would be an example to all the other slave owners that they must do the same. As for Pierce, was he not hoping that once his wife saw how kind and humane the operation of the slave system was, her never-ending criticism of it would cease? Each had always expected to change the other's point of view. Now perhaps there was a chance to mend for good this jagged rent in their marriage.

On December 21, 1838, a Friday, Pierce and Fanny Butler with Sally, who was two and a half, and little Fanny, still an infant in the arms of nurse Margery O'Brien, took a train from Philadelphia to Baltimore on the first lap of their thousand-mile journey. Fanny had resolved to keep a record of her residence on a Georgia plantation in the form of letters written but not sent to Elizabeth Sedgwick.

These would at last contain the truth about the practice of slavery in the American South.

CHAPTER 17

The Journey South

"I ADVANCE IT, therefore, as a suspicion only, that the blacks, whether originally a distinct race, or made distinct by time and circumstances, are inferior to the whites in the endowments both of body and mind." This was the reluctant conclusion of Thomas Jefferson, one of the most deeply profound and humane leaders in the history of the world, as set down in his *Notes on the State of Virginia*. A slave owner himself, he tried desperately to have legislation enacted that would abolish slavery throughout the United States. As we know, he failed. His view of the Negro was based on a people who were mainly slaves held in total ignorance. How could his estimate of them have been fair, even by one so single-mindedly committed to fairness?

That the Negro was physically and mentally inferior, Southern slave owners naturally found necessary to believe. It justified the practice of their "peculiar institution." The Negro, they said, was meant to be a slave. But Fanny Kemble found that many people in the North also believed the Negro to be inferior, pointing out how little progress Negroes had made even when they were free. Many Negroes, they said, seemed inclined to laziness and stupidity. They had no standards, no desire for self-improvement and probably never would have. To Fanny the answer to these charges seemed simple enough: how could these free Negroes better themselves when they had little or no education and when the whole concept of self-improvement had been deliberately crushed in their antecedents by the slave owners? Among every people there is a spirit handed down through the generations, qualities and drives that are passed through family lines like the torches in ancient Olympic races. But in the case of the Negro, his emotional heritage was degradation and despair and the feeling that nothing, *nothing* could better his lot. These feelings were only increased by the treatment Negroes received from Northerners, who, though they may have done away with slavery, still regarded black people, at best, as figures of fun; at worst, as untouchables to be segregated and never associated with. Dignity and a sense of personal worth, which are the spurs to self-improvement, were constantly undercut in the free Negro by the mockery, the thousand humiliations imposed on him by ordinary white people. Even so, by Fanny's day some Negroes had already made something of themselves—but against what odds!

As for the still-enslaved Southern Negro, wasn't his fate better, Harriet St. Leger wanted to know, than that of the Irish peasant in her native country? In the years when a mysterious blight came on the potato crop, the peasants had often starved to death and, if they failed to pay their rents, they were ruthlessly turned out of their huts and thrown off their few miserable acres to wander the countryside in total hopelessness. At least a slave was assured of food, clothing, a roof over his head.

Would the most abject Irish peasant exchange his lot and bind himself over as a slave? retorted Fanny. She thought not. In fact he would probably be outraged at the idea. A man's birthright was more precious "yet than the mess of potage for which he is told to exchange it because he is starving."

As to the idea that the Negro was inferior in mental capacity, a mere animal incapable of receiving intellectual instruction, why, she wondered, had laws been passed in the South making it a crime to teach a slave to read and write? Where was the *danger?* she asked with superb sarcasm. To which a slave owner such as her husband might have replied: the danger in educating a slave was that it stirred him up and made him unhappy. Since he could not advance to any extent equal with white men, was it not far more humane to leave him utterly debased, ignorant and unquestioning of the world and its ways?

All these arguments and counterarguments might well have raced through Fanny's head when on landing at Portsmouth, Virginia, on the morning of December 22, 1839, she saw for the first time a group of slaves. Nothing about their appearance added to her approval of "the peculiar institution" as slavery was so often termed. "They were poorly clothed; looked horribly dirty, and had a lazy recklessness in their air and manner as they sauntered along, which naturally belongs to creatures without one of the responsibilities which are the honorable burthen of rational humanity."

Fanny's journey south with her family, including the new baby whom she was still nursing, is an incredible record of the hardships of travel in the United States a mere century and a half ago. Let us follow her on her way:

At Philadelphia she had boarded a railway coach, violently overheated by a pot-bellied stove at one end, which passed through Wilmington, Delaware, and brought her to Havre de Grace in Maryland, where the Susquehanna River empties into the Chesapeake Bay. Here a boat able to cut through inch-thick ice with ease and swiftness landed the party on the opposite shore, where another train took them on to Baltimore. After an overnight boat journey (during which Fanny finished Charles Dickens' wonderful new novel *Oliver Twist*) the little party had climbed into another railroad car that carried them further south through swamplands that looked to Fanny's eyes "like some blasted region lying under an enchanter's ban, such as one reads of in old stories. Nothing lived nor moved throughout the lonesome solitude, and the sunbeams themselves seemed to sicken and grow pale as they glided like ghosts through these watery woods."

In the late afternoon they reached a knot of houses that was all that existed at the time of the town of Weldon, North Carolina. Here while they awaited the appearance of new cars from a branch line, the travelers freshened themselves at an inn provided by the railroad company and where Fanny was offered a meal of chicken "swimming in black grease." Everything, she noted, the food, the tablecloths, the clothes of the Negroes who served her, was filthy.

Around eight o'clock the new train appeared and her young children, asleep from exhaustion, were carried on to it. Just after midnight it came to an abrupt halt in the middle of thick woods. Peering out the window Fanny saw three four-horse carriages in a clearing waiting mysteriously by the light of a blazing pine bonfire. The train had gone as far as the track was laid, and now she must gather up her sleeping babies and board one of the vehicles that she detested so much and bump and sway and lurch for the rest of the night over a terrible corduroy road.

Sometime after dawn on Friday, they arrived at a crude hostelry that served the travelers a breakfast of "eggs, all begrimed with smoke and powdered with cinders, and some unbaked dough cut into little lumps by way of bread." When Fanny asked for a glass of milk it arrived "covered with dust and dirt, full of such sour stuff that I was obliged to put it aside."

The afternoon saw them at the Neuse River, which runs through the middle of North Carolina southeast to the sea. Here the passengers were made to get out and cross a high and rotten bridge on foot. Where the planks had dropped away Fanny could see the water far beneath as she clutched her baby in her arms. After the walkers had passed over, the coaches with their loads thus lightened followed on, one by one. Ten miles beyond the river the railway tracks suddenly began again, but there was no train waiting to meet them as scheduled. The sun had set and it became bitterly cold. There was nothing for the travelers to do but huddle in the unheated coaches and wait. Meanwhile a group of local people, the men dressed coarsely, but the women wearing pathetic bits of finery such as a pink bonnet or a blue artificial flower, gathered around and stared. They had really come to see the new-fangled railroad train, but meanwhile it was novelty enough to gawk at fine folk from the North. For Fanny there was an equal novelty in seeing the women chew and spit tobacco.

When the train still failed to appear someone remembered a farm nearby owned by a colonel who had fought in the Revolution. On hearing of their plight, he graciously asked in the passengers, allowed them to refresh themselves, produced bowls of milk for the babies and a supper of old cheese, bad butter, and dry biscuits for the adults at a price of fifty cents a head. Three hours later the train finally put in an appearance and at five o'clock the next morning the Butler party found itself in Wilmington, North Carolina, on the Fear River close to the sea. Here at the only hotel, Pierce was made to share a room with a fellow male passenger, while the women were allotted a chamber of their own. Fanny bedded down the infants with Margery and threw herself on a mattress on the floor and went fast asleep.

That evening the steamboat *Governor Dudley* set out on the overnight trip to Charleston, South Carolina, and this part of the journey for a wonder was clean and comfortable. Fanny slept the whole night through and only awoke as the boat rode into Charleston Harbor. It was now the morning of Christmas Day.

Fanny thought Charleston highly picturesque in contrast to most American towns where all the buildings seemed to have a characterless similarity that echoed the keen desire to conform that she had observed in many Americans. The steamboat *Wil-*

liam Seabrook would take them on to Savannah, but it ran only once a week so they were obliged to stop for two days at Charleston. On the first evening there Fanny heard a tolling of bells and the rumbling sound of drums—signals, so she learned, for the nightly curfew. No Negro was allowed out after nine o'clock without a pass. Fanny thought that the distant sounds seemed menacing and ominous.

Late on the evening of December 27 the Butler party set off again. Their boat, however, not being considered sturdy enough to go into the open sea, took a tedious inland route through a series of rivers and ocean inlets. The following day it stopped at Edisto Island, famed for producing America's finest cotton, and while the boat stayed at the landing Fanny went ashore and saw her first cotton gin in a nearby ginning house.

In a driving rainstorm they reached Savannah on the afternoon of December 29, where they at last found a decent hotel that even provided the luxury of a hot bath. At dinner, eaten at a common table, one of the other hotel guests, recognizing Fanny as an outsider and English, asked her how she liked the appearance of "our blackies—no want of cheerfulness, no despondency, no misery in their appearance, eh, Madame?" he added defensively. Fanny did not reply.

That evening a small, tidy little vessel called the *Ocmulgee* bore the Butler party away from Savannah still further south along the irregular coast of Georgia. The day dawned brilliantly, becoming clear and warm and the sun sparkled on the crisp-looking water. When the boat reached the mouth of the Altamaha River and turned into it everyone grew very excited. Pierce Butler's plantation was situated on Butler Island near one of the many arms of this wide, shallow seaway.

Along another of its arms stood the little town of Darien, and it was here that the *Ocmulgee* brought them. Just as it was tying up to the landing two other boats came alongside and a group of colored men shouted and waved: "Oh Massa, how you do, Massa? Oh, Missis! lily Missis! me glad to see you." For the first time Fanny beheld the slaves of Pierce Butler come to meet him and his family and escort them home.

One final lap of the journey remained, crossing through a canal from Darien and upriver to Butler Island. On the landing to greet the slave owner and his wife was a crowd of Negroes jumping, dancing, shouting, laughing, and clapping as the boat came in. Some seized parts of Fanny's clothing or kissed her hands, and one tall, gaunt Negro woman, bolder than the rest, threw her arms about Fanny and embraced her. Half frightened, Fanny made her way with her children through the milling throng to the safety of the house, and sinking onto a chair, burst into a fit of laughter as much out of nervousness as amusement at the antics of the slaves.

The journey to Georgia, which today would perhaps take three hours by plane, had lasted ten days. But Fanny was on a slave plantation at last.

CHAPTER 18

The Truth About Slavery

BUTLER ISLAND, not much more than two miles long, was shaped like a comma with a big head. The land lay below sea level and various tidal rivers surrounding it were kept out by a series of dikes and ditches. On the island were four slave settlements or camps—clusters of huts in which the Negro bondsmen lived. Mr. Butler possessed three mills to thresh the rice (for this was the crop of Butler Island). One ran by steam, another by horse-power, and the third worked through the force of the tide itself. There were also various outbuildings such as a blacksmith's shop, a cook's house from which food was doled out to the slaves, usually by the oldest female in each settlement. Finally there was the overseer's house, where Fanny was now to reside.

It contained three rooms, one for sitting and eating, another that was Pierce and Fanny's bedroom, and upstairs a room for Margery and the children. In addition there were three small cubicles, one of which served as a bedroom for the overseer, who lived with the Butlers like one of the family, another for his office, and a third as Pierce's dressing room–office. The kitchen was in a separate building. It had a dirt floor on which a number of Negroes were usually to be found crouching, hoping for a scrap of food to drop. Fanny did not go there any more than she could help, fearing permanently to lose her appetite. "Such being our abode," she commented dryly to Elizabeth Sedgwick, "I think you will allow there is little danger of my being dazzled by the luxurious splendors of a Southern slave residence."

Just before dawn the morning after she arrived the blowing of conch horns in the various slave camps sounded over the rice marshes and through the thickets of tall, green trees draped with ghostly Spanish moss. This was the signal, Fanny learned, for the Negroes to begin another day of enforced labor, the only kind of life they had ever known. Taking their food ration for the day, but without eating it, they went into the fields in teams under the supervision of a driver, himself a Negro slave, but who was empowered to keep his team working in an orderly and efficient fashion. In his hand he carried a whip, "a short stick of moderate size with a thick square leather thong attached to it," with which he was allowed to inflict a punishment of up to a dozen lashes, as he saw fit. The driver, however, was not privileged in any other way and could be punished by the same whip that he wielded or sold by his master like any of his fellow slaves.

Each man and woman on Butler Island, with the exception of the very old, Fanny learned, was given his "task" for the day by the driver—so many rows of rice field to rake, so much ditch to be cleaned. Before Pierce Butler had actually visited the estates that he and his brother had inherited from his grandfather, it had been customary to give the women slaves tasks equal to those of the men, but Pierce put a stop to this practice and ordered the work of the women to be diminished. The task was usually carefully worked out in relation to the ability of the one performing it so that except for a break at noon when the slaves ate their first meal of the day, heating up their rice and grits over fires in the place where they worked, it very often took until sundown to accomplish. Slaves who failed to complete their tasks were liable to a flogging; so were those who in their haste to finish for the day did their work carelessly. Usually darkness would be setting in by the time the laborers returned to their cabins, where, exhausted, they ate their second meal of the day and fell asleep. This was the existence of a slavehand on Butler Island—except on Sunday, when he did not work.

Other slaves did tasks of a different kind. They were the artisans, some of them highly skilled carpenters, who took great pride in their work, or coopers, who made the barrels but also the tools used on the plantation. Finally there were the house servants, considered the most privileged of all since they were at least exposed to the white people's civilized ways, some of which rubbed off on them, and who could expect precious tidbits of food or scraps of clothing to be flung their way. For such a tiny house only five servants were required in addition to the baby's Irish nurse, Margery—and of these Fanny tried whenever she could to do without the services of the two lads, in their teens, who were supposed to act as footmen. So filthy were their faces, hands, and bare feet, that the smell of them was almost too much to bear.

That the Negro had a peculiar body smell was a prevalent and wide-spread idea, yet remembering the stench of the poor Irish or Scotch when she sometimes visited their hovels, Fanny wrote Elizabeth Sedgwick in her usual perceptive way: "I am strongly inclined to believe that peculiar ignorance of the laws of health and habits of decent cleanliness are the real and only causes of this disagreeable characteristic."

A day or two after her arrival Fanny was summoned to the porch of her little home to find waiting the tall, emaciated Negro woman who had embraced her when she first arrived. The woman's name was Teresa, and she explained that she had borne a large number of children and with the long, hard tasks imposed on her every day in the fields she had suffered a kind of rupture. Suddenly holding up the skirt of her coarse woolen dress that was her only garment, she showed her body to Fanny's horrified eyes, which saw only too plainly the truth of what the woman had said. Promising to try to intercede so that Teresa's field tasks would be lightened, Fanny sent her to the infirmary saying that she would get remedies for her ailments as soon as possible.

Soon afterward Fanny set out to visit the infirmary located at the end of a row of slave quarters in back of her own house, first stopping in a cabin, to see what one was like. The hut consisted of a single room perhaps twelve by fifteen, partitioned at one side into two cubicles that served as bedrooms. Each compartment contained a crude bedstead with a mound of Spanish moss for a mattress and vermin-ridden blankets as covering. Two families, sometimes as many as eight or more in each, shared the cabin, which was attached to a clumsy outside chimney. Adjoining the building was a patch of ground supposed to be used for a garden but generally neglected.

As to the condition of the slave cabin: "Instead of the order, neatness and ingenuity, which might convert these miserable hovels into tolerable residences, there was the careless, reckless, filthy indolence which even the brutes do not exhibit in their lairs and nests. . . . Firewood and shavings lay littered about the floors, while the half-naked children were cowering around two or three smoldering cinders.

"In the midst of the floor or squatting round the cold hearth would be four or five little children from four to ten years old, the latter all with babies in their arms, the care of the infants being taken from the mothers (who are driven afield as soon as they recover from child labor) and devolved upon these poor little nurses, as they are called, whose business it is to watch the infant, and carry it to its mother whenever it may require nourishment."

Passing down the "street" between the slave cabins Fanny came to a larger two-story building of whitewashed wood containing four rooms. This was the infirmary. Fanny opened the door to the first room and stood speechless with horror, while the full impact of the dreadfulness of slavery, all that she had imagined it to be, now washed over her. "In the enormous chimney glimmered the powerless embers of a few sticks of wood around which, however, as many of the sick women as could approach it were cowering, some on wooden settles, most of them on the ground, excluding those who were too ill to rise; and these last poor wretches lay prostrate on the floor, without bed, mattress or pillow, buried in tattered and filthy blankets. . . . Here, in their hour of sickness and suffering, lay those whose health and strength are spent in unrequited labor for us—those whose husbands, fathers, brothers and sons were even at that hour sweating over the earth whose produce was to buy for us all the luxuries which health can revel in, all the comforts which can alleviate sickness. I stood in the midst of them unable to speak, the tears pouring from my eyes at this sad spectacle of their misery, myself and my emotion alike strange and incomprehensible to them.

"Here lay women expecting every hour the terrors and agonies of childbirth, others who had just brought their doomed offspring into the world; . . . here lay some burning with fever, others chilled with cold and aching with rheumatism upon the hard, cold ground, the draughts and dampness increasing their sufferings, and dirt, noise and stench and every aggravation of which sickness is capable, combined in their condition—here they lay like brute beasts, absorbed in physical suffering. . . . Now pray take notice that this is the hospital of an estate where the owners are supposed to be humane, the overseers efficient and kind, and the Negroes remarkably well cared for and comfortable."

Recovering herself, Fanny went to work. She ordered Rose, the midwife in charge of the dark room, to open the shutters that had been drawn against the cold because few of the windows had glass panes, while she herself started to make up the fire. As she snatched up a log there was a horrified outcry: "Let alone, Missis—let be; what for you lift wood?" Together the two women, the one who had been the idolized actress of the English-speaking world, the most celebrated star of her time, the other a pathetic, illiterate slave, worked side by side to clean up the disgusting room, clearing out the rubbish and filth from the floor, folding the piles of ragged blankets not in use and moving some of the patients into more comfortable positions. In the room was a mother excused from her task in the field to nurse her ill baby. When Fanny reproved her for the infant's filthy condition the woman, named Harriet, replied that working from dawn to dusk as they did, she and mothers like her were too tired to do anything but fling themselves down to eat and sleep.

From this room Fanny went on to the adjoining one and to those upstairs used by the sick men. Everywhere were the same loathsome conditions, even worse for the men—as they had no beds at all, but lay helplessly on the floor under their tattered coverings. Her clothes covered with dirt and vermin, Fanny rushed back to the house and burst out at her husband. Disheveled, the famous Kemble eyes flashing, the famous Kemble voice cracking with emotion, she described the horrors of what she had seen and cried out—did Pierce have no *conscience?*

The overseer who was also present, and amazed that a woman could and would speak to her husband so critically, put in an explanation. The previous year when he had taken over his job from the former overseer, Mr. Roswell King, Jr., he had proposed to Mr. King and John Butler, brother of Pierce Butler, that they renovate the infirmary and equip it properly. Since neither man had responded to the idea he had left it in the condition in which he had found it, and in which it had been for nineteen years under Mr. King, a man whose management of the Butler estates had returned a full income from them. Such efficient overseers, as Fanny well knew, had no interest in slaves who were sick and could not work.

Bitterly, Fanny continued to upbraid her husband for allowing such unspeakable conditions to exist among the very people who labored to support him in luxury, while the overseer listened, more and more amazed. Never had he heard a woman speak her mind so freely, so boldly—above all, to the man who was her husband. What kind of a man was Mr. Butler to allow himself to be humiliated by his wife in front of his employee? Carried away by her outraged feelings, Fanny next turned on the overseer and angrily reproached him for imposing tasks that took so long to accomplish that mothers like Harriet did not have time to care for their babies.

The overseer was furious at being spoken to thus by a woman. He would show her what kind of a man he was. The next day Fanny learned that he had ordered Harriet, still ill herself, taken from her sick baby in the infirmary. Stripping her back bare, he had personally flogged her.

CHAPTER 19

Fanny Fights Back

"I REALLY NEVER was so busy in all my life as I am here," Fanny wrote a few weeks later in her journal-letter for Elizabeth Sedgwick. "No time, no place affords me a respite from my innumerable petitioners; and whether I be asleep or awake, reading, eating or walking—in the kitchen, my bedroom, or the parlor—they flock in with urgent entreaties and pitiful stories. . . . Surely the least I can do is to hear these, my most injured benefactors; and indeed, so intense in me is the sense of injury they receive from me and mine, that I should scarce dare refuse the very clothes from my back or food from my plate if they asked me for it."

There was little—pitifully little—that she could do; a bit of flannel to dress a new-born baby, soap—"If Missis only give we, we be so clean forever"—sugar and rice to augment their meager diet. Her main project was the infirmary. Here she nursed the sick, very often relieving their suffering simply by washing the grime off their bodies. Day by day she made the place cleaner, warmer, and more comfortable, giving its inmates an all-important sense of being looked after, something they had never known before. Finally by pleading with Pierce she obtained his promise of new beds, mattresses, pillows, and blankets. A new story would be added onto the building for the sickest patients. Fanny was jubilant. Even if she could do little, every tiny improvement in the lot of the slaves, whether it was merely seeing that one of the new babies was bathed and clothed by her own hand, seemed to her a step forward to civilization for these people who had been so relentlessly denied it.

But for every tiny accomplishment there was a monstrous injustice to match it. She asked Pierce to speak to the overseer about the flogging of Harriet because the slave had complained to Fanny of her long work day. That was not the reason he had punished her, claimed the overseer: Mrs. Butler must not believe the word of any of the slaves. They were all liars. The truth was that when he had ordered Harriet into the fields she had said that she was ill and could not work. Since he knew she was lying he had repeated the command and she had replied: "Very well, I'll go but I'll just come back again."

"For this reply," said the overseer, "I gave her a good lashing; it was her business to have gone into the field without answering me and then we should have seen whether she would work or not."

As we look back on the practice of slavery in the American South we can see now that it was the least efficient labor system possible. Naturally, slaves tried to work slow or feign illness, which is what the overseer suspected of Harriet. What incentive had slaves to want to work at all? Their one and only luxury under the terms their existence imposed on them was idleness.

As the days passed Fanny began to find out some of the disastrous effects slavery was having on the South. One night at dinner the Butlers had a visitor, Mr. Roswell King, Jr., the former overseer whom Fanny dreaded meeting, ever since learning that he was the one responsible for the condition of the infirmary, even though he was known to be an honorable, capable man, who had for nineteen years single-handedly ruled over seven hundred slaves. After dinner Mr. King talked interestingly about the farmers of Georgia who had small amounts of land as opposed to the large holdings of the plantation owners. Because labor was considered to be the lot of the slaves only, these so-called "poor whites" imitated the rich and idle plantation owners, even though not having slaves of their own they could ill afford to do so. As a result their farms were miserable, run-down affairs, scarcely kept up at all. Still poorer white men existed who owned no land at all, but refusing to work (only slaves did work) simply squatted in the pine woods or swamp lands that belonged to others, and lived by shooting wildfowl or deer or stealing from nearby plantation gardens. As ignorant as the blacks, they were not even subject to the slight moral and religious standards imposed on the slaves. Indeed many slaves of rich masters looked down on the "po' white trash" and mocked the tattered squalor of these brutal, derelict people. At least "massa" looked after his slaves and saw to their well-being. Feeling the contempt of the Negroes, the poor whites, despising themselves and the degraded way in which they lived, despised the Negroes more. This hatred has continued to this day, eating like some savage pest at the heart of America, and it can be directly attributed to the practice of slavery in the South.

"The whole machinery of slavery was so constructed as to cause labor, as a rule, to be looked upon as a badge of degradation, of inferiority. . . . The slave system . . . in a large measure, took the spirit of self-reliance and self-help out of the white people." These words are from the remarkable autobiography, *Up From Slavery,* by Booker T. Washington, a man born a slave who founded Tuskegee Institute, the first college for Negroes in America. He wrote them in 1901. Fanny saw the truth of what slavery was doing to the white people as well as the Negroes in 1839.

Of the "institution" Fanny was startled to hear Mr. King, a shrewd and clever man, who had lived all his life among slaves, say: "I hate slavery with all my heart; I consider it an absolute curse wherever it exists. It will keep those states where it does exist fifty years behind the others in improvement and prosperity." Then he added, "As for its being an irremediable evil—a thing not to be helped or got rid of—that's all nonsense; for, as soon as people become convinced that it is in their interest to get rid of it, they will soon find the means to do so, depend on it."

Then why couldn't slavery be abolished? Fanny wondered. This was a humanitarian age when people would "not long endure what they perceive to be injurious to their fortunes and advancement." If the majority of Southerners saw the evils of slavery why did they not do away with it? "I'll tell you why abolition is impossible," said Mr. King, "because every healthy Negro can fetch a thousand dollars in the Charleston market at this moment." As long as slaves remained immensely valuable the system would stay. Fanny's very own daughters, Sally and little Fanny, were among the wealthiest heiresses in America, but if Mr. Butler freed his slaves they would be penniless. Hired laborers could never be found to work on these fetid, malaria-ridden plantations.

Another iniquity of the system of slavery deeply troubling to Fanny was the whole problem of families and family life among the Negroes. "Marriages" of a kind existed among the slaves, though these were not legal since a slave had no legal rights of any kind. Many of the men and women had loose morals—how could they have otherwise, since the slave owners were not averse to promiscuity among their bondsmen? Loose morals promised babies that one day would grow into valuable slaves. Again, directly attributable to slavery, came the stereotype, handed down until recently, that the Negro people are immoral.

One way for a slave woman to gain favor in the eyes of her master was to present him with a number of babies—future slaves—and some became mothers as young as thirteen or fourteen. Also when they became pregnant their work load was usually lightened; they were given extra rations of food and clothing and after their confinement could count on at least three weeks of taking care of the baby, before returning to the fields. Fanny thought this period of recovery after childbirth not long enough and constantly implored Pierce to lengthen it at least to a month. Because of the endless bending and lifting of weight involved in their work, many women, Fanny learned from slave mothers, lost more than half of their babies through miscarriages or stillbirths.

"I've lost a many; they all goes so," one mother repeated to her in a flat voice. There was a strange fatality to her manner, an acceptance of the taking away of life as well as the giving of it that has been handed down to the Negro women of this day. Nor is it surprising. In March, 1968, the *New York Times* reported that the incidence of infant mortality among Negroes in the United States is still three times more than whites.

After twelve or fifteen births the bodies of many slave women like Teresa were broken. Finding Fanny, unlike most of the Southern women with whom they might usually have come in contact, strangely sympathetic to their problems, the female slaves asked her to intercede that their work loads be lightened. Again and again Fanny appealed to Pierce, who usually refused her requests, pointing out that the only way a profit could be wrung from the plantation was to make the slaves work, not to pay to keep them idle. Fanny felt helpless. If one accepted the system then what Pierce said was only common sense. *If one accepted the system*. But how could he? she asked herself, when every day he witnessed scenes of gross injustice—barbarities for which he was entirely responsible. What kind of a man had she married? Fanny began to wonder.

One evening Mr. Butler was called out to hear a complaint from a gang of pregnant women who claimed that they were overworked. As he stood on the porch telling them it was their duty to do the tasks allotted to them, a wave of shame overcame Fanny, and Pierce suddenly seemed to her positively "degraded and unmanly. How honorable he would have appeared to me begrimed with the sweat and soil of the coarsest manual labor," she wrote in her journal-letter to Elizabeth Sedgwick. "I turned away in bitter disgust."

Wider and wider became the rift that the sharp-edged blade of slavery cut between husband and wife.

One of the worst fears among closely knit slave families was that they might be put up for sale and husband and wife separated, or the children taken from their mother and sent from all that was familiar to some place totally strange and new. One day Margery O'Brien referred to Fanny a curious question that she had been asked by the nursemaid who assisted her, a mulatto named Psyche. The slave, a gentle, melancholy girl just over twenty, had wanted to know if Margery knew by any chance who owned her and her two children. When Fanny sought out Psyche to learn why she had asked the question, the young woman tremblingly explained that she was Mr. King's property. The former overseer, who had been visiting Butler Island, had bought a plantation further west and was about to move his slaves onto it. Would she and her two children be taken from her husband, Joe, a fine and intelligent slave owned by Mr. Butler? Or by any chance had Mr. Butler purchased her? For days Psyche had been living in dread and suspense, not knowing her fate.

Fanny calmed the girl and said she would find out right away who owned her. If Mr. Butler had not yet bought Psyche and her children, Fanny would see to it that he did. At the end of the day Mr. Butler was still out when the overseer came into the house that he shared with the Butler family. At once Fanny asked him if he knew who owned Psyche. To her surprise the man replied that he did. Mr. King, thinking that she would be troublesome to him where he was going in Alabama (all slaves dreaded being sent to the new cottonlands of the Southwest where their hardships were even greater) had offered Psyche and her children to him for sale. "And so as I had no objection to investing a little money that way I bought them."

Fanny rushed to Psyche with the welcome news that she would not be sent away. But the slave girl with her sad, grave eyes and butter-colored skin was still doubtful. If Mr. Butler would only purchase her then the whole family would be owned by one man and she would be relieved in her own mind.

The next morning as Fanny was dressing, she heard coming from Mr. Butler's office a frenzied voice shaking with sobs. The cries of despair increased to such an extent that Fanny could no longer control herself and threw open the connecting door. There on his knees before Mr. Butler was Joe, Psyche's husband, begging, pleading, imploring him not to send him away from his parents, his wife and children and the only home he had ever known. It seemed that Mr. Butler had been so pleased with Mr. King's excellent management of his estates for nineteen years that he had given him Joe as a present, and now Mr. King was planning to take Joe west to his new plantation in dreaded Alabama. As Joe continued his piteous pleas, Mr. Butler stood over him, leaning against a table, his arms folded implacably and finally told the slave to stop trying to change what could not be helped. Fanny, her heart throbbing, her breath coming in little gasps, turned away from the sight of her immovable husband and shut the door.

Was it still possible for her to intercede with Pierce? Did the passionate devotion that he had once shown for her, which had led him to pursue her doggedly—*slavishly*—until she was his, still have any power over him? Or had some strange effect from owning slaves come over him and hardened his heart to all that was human? Fanny went to Pierce and began to plead—as Joe had pleaded. She stormed, she wept, begging him to save himself from committing an act so utterly inhuman. Mr. Butler remained completely silent.

That evening the overseer came into the sitting room where Fanny was sewing. The only subject on her mind, Fanny immediately asked, "Have you seen Joe this afternoon?"

"Yes, ma'am; he's a great deal happier than he was this morning."

"Why, how is that?"

"Oh he's not going to Alabama. Mr. King heard that he had kicked up a fuss about it and said that if the fellow wasn't willing to go with him, he did not wish to be bothered with any Negroes down there who were to be troublesome, so he might as well stay behind."

"And does Psyche know this?"

"Yes, ma'am. I suppose so."

Fanny drew a long breath of relief. Joe, Psyche, the two clean, neatly cared for children were safe, at least for the moment. She sat thinking over the whole situation, her husband's behavior in it, and for the first time felt a strange, choking guilt that it was her own fault as well, even though when she had married Pierce Butler she had not the slightest knowledge that he owned human beings as property.

The next day Pierce maintained a broad silence on the subject of Joe and Psyche, much to Fanny's impatience. She was eager to unite the slave family by persuading Mr. Butler to purchase Psyche and her children from the overseer. That evening she again found herself alone with this squint-eyed, slow-moving man with whom she now so curiously shared her home. New thoughts spilled through Fanny's head. Perhaps she herself could buy Psyche and her children by selling the jewelry that she owned. How much was each of her necklaces, her pairs of earrings worth? she wondered. Ironically, she thought back to her days as an actress when with such ease she had earned thousands of dollars. How she wished she could go on the stage now. Finally, unable to contain herself any longer, Fanny blurted out to the overseer: "I have a particular favor to beg of you. Promise me that you will never sell Psyche and her children without first letting me know of your intention to do so, and giving me the option of buying them."

The overseer slowly laid down the book he was reading. "Dear me, ma'am, I'm very sorry—I have sold them." Fanny's sewing fell from her lap and her mouth opened wide, but in her dismay she could not get out a single word. "I didn't know, ma'am, you see, at all," the overseer mumbled, "that you entertained any idea of making an investment of that nature; for I'm sure if I had, I would willingly have sold the woman to you; but I sold her and her children this morning to Mr. Butler."

With a glad cry Fanny rushed from the room to find Pierce and thank him. Then did he love her still as much? Even more important, was he beginning to see that she was right about slavery?

CHAPTER 20

Disillusion

WHATEVER HOPES she may have had were quickly dashed. "I am told that a total change in my opinions on slavery was anticipated from my residence on a plantation," Fanny wrote bitterly to a friend in England from Butler Island on January 30, 1839, "a statement which only convinces me that one may live in the most intimate relations with one's fellow creatures and really know nothing about them after all."

The comment, it should be pointed out, worked both ways. If Pierce Butler thought foolishly that he might change Fanny's opinions on slavery, was not Fanny just as foolish to think that she could persuade him to her point of view? With an increasingly silent, almost menacing air he would listen to her intercessions on behalf of some of the overworked slaves and might reluctantly see that their work load was lightened. And she gained a small victory over the improvement of the infirmary. But there was still no change in the former overseer's practice of sending the women back to work only three weeks after their confinements. As for the basic issue of slavery itself and the unassailable wrong of it she made no headway with Pierce Butler at all, though by raising the issue so repeatedly she angered him more and more.

One day, Teresa, the tall, gaunt woman who had complained to Fanny of being overworked accosted her and told her that she had been flogged by the driver of the gang for having come to Fanny. Fanny, horrified, went to her husband, who told her that Teresa had been given the usual punishment for not having done her task. This was the law. The fact that Fanny was on the island and felt sorry for the lot of the slaves could not be allowed to undermine their discipline, he added coldly. If Teresa chose to take time away from the field to appeal to Fanny when she should have been working then she must take the consequences and receive her just punishment.

Just? burst out Fanny, unable, as always, to control herself. Was unpaid, enforced labor *just?* Was allowing a man to strip and lash a woman, the mother of ten children, just? Was it just that Teresa's toil should maintain two idle young brothers in luxury? In her passion she forgot herself: was it manly, she asked tauntingly, that a man should allow himself to be supported by the work of women, women whom he cruelly abused as well?

There was a silence. Mr. Butler loomed over his wife, his handsome, indolent face showing no expression whatsoever. Then he turned away. The conversation, he said, he found disagreeable.

The days passed. Fanny was witness to many remarkable sights in her strange existence on the slave plantation. "Often in the evening," she told Elizabeth Sedgwick, ". . . [as] I sit writing this daily history for your edification, the door of the room is opened stealthily and one after another, men and women come trooping silently in, their naked feet falling all but inaudibly on the bare boards as they betake themselves to the hearth, where they squat down on their hams in a circle, the bright blaze from the huge pine log, which is the only light of this half of the room, shining on their sooty limbs and faces. . . . You cannot imagine anything stranger than the effect of all these glassy whites of eyes and grinning white teeth turned toward me, and shining in the flickering light. I very often take no notice of them at all, and they seem perfectly absorbed in contemplating me. My evening dress probably excites their wonder and admiration no less than my rapid and continuous writing, for which they have sometimes expressed compassion, as if they thought it must be more laborious than hoeing; sometimes at the end of my day's journal I look up and say suddenly, 'Well, what do you want?' when each black figure springs up at once, as if moved by machinery; they all answer, 'Me come say ha do (how d'ye do), Missis'; and they troop out as noiselessly as they entered."

On another occasion a valuable slave named Shadrach was stricken with pneumonia, and like most of the slaves living in the damp, noxious climate on a poor diet, he had no resistance to disease and quickly died. The funeral was held at dusk by the light of flaring torches, and Fanny and Pierce stood among the mourners, all eyes upon them as the objects of wonderment and admiration. The service began with a hymn in which all the high, wailing voices joined in haunting unison. Then the self-appointed clergyman, an intelligent slave named London who was one of the coopers on the plantation and who had learned to read, began a prayer. All the slaves knelt on the moist earth and Fanny too. Only Mr. Butler stood unyieldingly alone.

In his prayer, London asked God's blessings on the slaves' master and mistress and Fanny began to cry. After the prayer the coffin was taken to the slaves' burial ground and when London had finished speaking to the assembly on the subject of Lazarus and the raising of the dead, the coffin was lowered into the grave which had half filled with water, Butler Island being lower than the sea rivers that surround it. This dismayed the slaves and for the first time they broke their dignified silence with cries of sorrow and fear. Their chief concern, however, was for Fanny's tears. "God bless you, Missis!" they exclaimed as Fanny and Pierce said good-night and turned in the direction of the house. "Lor, Missis, don't you cry so." Pierce sent the torchbearers to their quarters, and husband and wife walked home by the light of the stars in the lovely deep blue sky, while the tears continued to stream down Fanny's cheeks.

Ever her energetic self, in the time when Fanny was not occupied with the demands of either her own children or those of the slaves, she explored the island. Walking was limited to the dikes that surrounded the swampy, oozy land, so she decided to teach herself to row, traveling always in the company of a quick, intelligent youth in his teens named Jack, who acted as her personal servant, while she explored the intricate patterns of the alligator-infested Altamaha River. This is how she described the appearance of the country to Harriet St. Leger:

"Right and left, as the eye follows the broad and brimming surface of this vast body of turbid water, it rests on nothing but low swamplands where the rattling sedges like a tawny forest of reeds make warm winter shelters for the snakes and alligators, which the summer sun will lure in scores from their lurking places; or hoary woods upon whose straggling upper boughs, all hung with gray mosses like disheveled hair, the bald-headed eagle swoops from the sky. . . . All this looks wild enough; and as the peculiar light of the Southern sunset falls upon the scene, I almost expect to see the canoes of the red men shoot from the banks, which were so lately the possession of his race alone."

One day while out rowing she started up a flock of birds from a low swamp, which in their flight for a few seconds darkened the sun. Again Fanny remembered Aunt Whitelock's stories of life in the United States, and how the family had scoffed and refused to believe her.

Occasionally Fanny would go shopping in the ramshackle town of Darien, having, as everywhere else, to take a boat to reach it. One day while there she heard being discussed a project called the Brunswick Canal, designed to put the city of Brunswick, Georgia, south of Darien, in more direct contact with the Atlantic Ocean. It was to be built partly by Irish laborers paid at the rate of twenty dollars a month, the rest by slave gangs hired out by their owners. This practice of renting out slaves seemed the most frightful of any that Fanny had heard yet. The hirers of the slaves would of course feel no responsibility toward them, merely wanting to get their money's worth of labor out of them. What cruel lengths would they not go to obtain it?

As February came on the weather began to warm in these damp, subtropical lands where no white man stayed after March, fearing the fevers of malaria. For three quarters of a year the rice plantation was then entirely under the supervision of the Negro boss driver, Frank. It seems extraordinary that some of the slaves during this period did not attempt to escape. Yet where could they go? All around was the same treacherous, oozing land infested with alligators and poisonous snakes. One female slave told Fanny that she had run away after a brutal flogging only to come back more dead than alive from hunger and exposure. There was no place to go and no one, no one at all to help a runaway slave.

Toward the end of February Pierce Butler went fifteen miles downriver to another of his estates, this one a cotton plantation on St. Simon's Island, where he prepared to bring his wife and family in a few days' time. Fanny found herself once again alone with the squint-eyed overseer and inevitably the conversation turned to the subject of slavery. She asked him if any of her husband's slaves could read and he replied, happily, only a few.

Had he observed insubordination in those who did know their letters? she wanted to know, thinking how loyal and excellent a slave was London, the cooper who had conducted Shadrach's funeral service.

"I don't say whether it's right or wrong," began the overseer speaking, to Fanny's surprise, of slavery itself, but if the practice were to continue, he went on, then every step that a slave took toward enlightenment the more difficult it would be to control him. Therefore in his opinion it was better that slaves did not learn to read. The logic of this argument Fanny could not deny—

logic, however, always, *always* based on acceptance of the system of slavery.

To her even greater surprise the overseer then went on to say that he believed free labor would be more profitable on the plantations than the work of slaves, which, since it was compulsory, "was of the worst possible quality and the smallest possible quantity." The costs of feeding and clothing the slaves were considerable, and in addition there were the totally wasted expenses of maintaining slaves too old or too young to work at all. Mr. Butler's Southern overseer, Fanny concluded, was as much in favor of freeing the slaves as any abolitionist!

A few days later all the family's personal belongings together with pots, pans, bedding, and various kinds of livestock were packed aboard the pretty plantation boat, *Lily,* manned by eight slaves at the oars, and the Butler family bade farewell to the rice plantation. The day before leaving Fanny had had an interesting talk with London, who asked her to send him a number of Bibles when she returned North. She was extremely curious as to how he had learned to read and did all in her power to find out. London's answers were always evasive: "Well, Missis, me learn . . . Well, Missis, me s'pose Heaven help me."

After a fifteen-mile row downstream, the *Lily* turned into a narrow channel deviating from the broad main course of the Altamaha. A few minutes later one of the slaves stood up in the bow of the boat and blew his conch horn, signaling their arrival on St. Simon's Island where the famous, long-staple Sea Island cotton was grown.

Here Fanny moved into a half-decayed, rotting farmhouse

where none of the doors shut tight and wind under the floorboards caused parts of the carpet to rise in little puffs. But at least there were stately live oaks, and close to the house narcissus and jonquils in bloom and two peach trees also in full flower. The air blowing across the island from the Atlantic was fresh and invigorating, unlike the fetid atmosphere of the rice plantation, and it occurred to Fanny that the island was big enough for her to indulge in her favorite form of exercise—horseback riding.

The conditions of the slaves seemed worse to her than on Butler Island, their quarters even more tumble down, the infirmary unspeakable. Fanny was besieged with the usual requests for a length of flannel, a quantity of sugar, some liniment to ease the aches of rheumatism. There were also the usual pleas from the women to have their tasks shortened—though they were less arduous than on the other plantation. Once again came the unfailing demands from the mothers of the newborn not to be sent back to the fields so soon after their confinements. If only they could have a month, one whole month to recover.

Again, as she had so many times before, Fanny tried to intercede for them with her husband. But now the blow fell. Angrily Pierce Butler told her that she was not to bother him any more with the slaves' complaints. Most of them were lies, just as the stories they were telling her about the oppressions of Mr. Roswell King, Jr., the former overseer, were lies. "Why do you believe such trash?" he demanded harshly. "Don't you know the niggers are all damned liars?"

Seated before her letter-journal the lines wrinkled and smeared before Fanny's tear-filled eyes. "I must return to the North," she wrote to Elizabeth Sedgwick, "for my condition would be almost worse than theirs—condemned to hear and see so much wretchedness, not only without the means of alleviating it, but without permission even to represent it for alleviation; this is no place for me, since I was not born among slaves, and cannot bear to live among them."

CHAPTER 21

One Person's Influence

IT HAD ALWAYS been Fanny's first reaction when feeling oppressed to run away. Once she had done it as a child but had been caught and severely punished. Now, the difference was, she could not. A grown woman, above all a mother, she could not abandon her babies but must remain on the plantation, as she put in her journal, "to learn this dreary lesson of human suffering to the end." Now when the petitioners came she was still able to give them the bandages, the ointments, the rice and sugar for which they were so pathetically grateful. But when the women came entreating, "Oh, Missis, you speak to Massa for us. Oh, Missis, you tell Massa for we, he sure do as you say," she could only turn away trying to hide her tears from these unhappy beings whose plight moved her so.

One day when a group of women appeared with the usual request for at least a month's rest after childbirth Fanny had to grip the table in front of her to control herself. Mr. Butler, she explained, would not let her bring their complaints to him. They must go to him themselves at a time when she was also with him and complain directly. Then perhaps she could urge their cause. With a heavy heart she dismissed the group, which shuffled out murmuring, "Oh yes, Missis, you will, you will speak to Massa for we; God bless you, Missis, we sure you will."

"I had my cry out for them, for myself, for *us,*" she wrote to Elizabeth Sedgwick. "All these women had had large families, and *all* of them had lost half their children, and several of them had lost more. How I do ponder upon the strange fate that has brought me here, from so far away, from surroundings so curiously different—how my own people in that blessed England of my birth would marvel if they could suddenly have a vision of me as I sit here, and how sorry some of them would be for me."

As Fanny traveled about on horseback talking to the slaves in their various settlements she heard from all sides sickening stories of the long hours, the severe punishments for tasks not done and other merciless means that Mr. Roswell King, Jr., had employed to get a rich profit out of the plantation. Fanny noticed too, that here were many more mulattos than on Butler Island. Some of them were actually offspring of Mr. King himself. The one slave whom the overseer had trusted and respected above all others was the boss driver, Frank, whom he had not hesitated to leave in charge of Butler Island during the malaria season. Yet, Fanny learned, he had also not hesitated to "borrow" Frank's wife, Betty, by whom he had had a son. Even more horrifying was the story of two other female slaves, both just delivered of children sired by Mr. King, who had been ordered out of the infirmary to be flogged and exiled to a penal section of the island by Mr. King's jealous wife.

The days dragged on. Fanny felt ill and depressed. Her one consolation was to be able to go riding and enjoy the beautiful scenery of St. Simon's Island, though fearful of the rattlesnakes that were everywhere, she rarely dismounted. She asked some of the young and willing slaves to cut trails through the forests for her, paying them to do the work after they had finished their tasks for the day, thus demonstrating how the system of paid labor worked. On this project she wrote to a friend in England:

"I wish I could for an instant cause a vision to rise before you of the perfect paradise of evergreens through which I have been opening paths on our estate, in an island called St. Simon's lying half in the sea and half in the Altamaha. Such noble growth of dark-leafed, wide-spreading oaks; such exquisite natural shrubberies of magnolia, wild myrtle and bay, all glittering evergreens of various tints, bound together by trailing garlands of wild jessamine, whose yellow bells, like tiny gold cups, exhale a perfume like that of the heliotrope and fill the air with sweetness and cover the woods with perfect curtains of bloom . . . while close to the earth clings a perfect carpet of thick-growing green, almost like moss, bearing clusters of little white blooms like enameled stars."

Sometimes she rode across the island to the Atlantic pounding on the sand beach where she gazed east across the water toward England and Europe. England! How remote it seemed. England! Her mother now buried in its earth, her father growing old and infirm. Who would take care of Adelaide if anything happened to him? Fortunately, her Paris debut had been a success, and Fanny had received word that she had gone on to new triumphs, singing in the lovely opera house, La Fenice, at Venice—a building that stands to this day. Everyone predicted that with her lovely voice and supreme dramatic talent, worthy of a Kemble, Adelaide would become the greatest prima donna of her time.

Opera . . . Society . . . Women in beautiful dresses, wearing glittering jewelry and delicious perfumes . . . One of Fanny's occasional occupations was to cut out and fit a dress of low-quality cotton for one of the slave women. Ordinarily they were issued a crude dress made like a shift that they used, without ever washing the garment, till it wore out. That March of 1839 a more exciting challenge was suddenly presented to Fanny. Aleck, an intelligent youth of sixteen who waited on table, suddenly came to her and humbly asked if she thought she could teach him to read. As he well knew, it would be against the law for her to do so, Fanny said cautiously that she would have to think about it. Inwardly, the head-strong impetuous Fanny of old had already made her decision. Since the law prescribed a heavy fine for anyone teaching a slave to read and write, she reasoned with some bitterness that Mr. Butler would have to pay it since he was entirely responsible for his wife's debts. Indeed, as a married woman, she had come to feel that she had very few rights more than the slaves she pitied so. Without rights what harm was there in behaving in what some might have condemned as an irresponsible way, particularly toward her husband? Unfortunately time was short. Mr. Butler had begun to talk of returning to the

North, and though invariably he never managed to get off on a journey when he said he would, Fanny would still have to hurry.

"I wonder if I shall come back again!" she mused to her journal, "and whether, when I do, I shall find the trace of one idea of a better life left in these poor people's minds by my sojourn among them." She was a woman, however, and like all people with a heart, possessed unbounded, inspiring faith. "To our children, our servants, our friends, our acquaintances—to each and all every day, and all day long, we are distributing that which is best or worst in existence—influence: with every word, with every look, with every gesture, something is given or withheld that may be of great importance, to the receiver, of inestimable importance, to the giver."

What would most hinder the development of the Negro people in America she saw readily: "The mode in which they have learned to accept the idea of their own degradation and unalterable inferiority is the most serious impediment I see in the way of their progress."

The last days of March came on. The weather turned springlike and a neighboring plantation owner sent over delicious peas from his garden. Fanny had been able to give Aleck several reading lessons, combining his instruction with that of her little fair-haired daughter Sally, who would, as matters stood then, one day be his owner. Though Fanny felt cruelly limited in what she could do for the slaves, there were still opportunities to show kindness. One evening a decrepit, rheumatic old woman named Dorcas came to ask for sugar and sank down exhausted from having had to walk clear across the island. She was preparing to walk back when Fanny said she would not let her and took the woman in her wagon even though the stench of the unwashed slave on the seat beside her was almost unbearable. Just as they had started out Dorcas noticed Fanny's watch on the table and pointing to it said: "Ah, I need not look at this; I have almost done with time." Fanny was struck by the poetic observation from one that most people would have dismissed as old and stupid.

By the middle of April the Butler family had begun to get ready to leave. Spring had clothed everything in its loveliest array: "The acacias are swinging their silver censers under the green roof of these wood temples; every stump is like a classical altar to the sylvan gods, garlanded with flowers. . . . Beautiful butterflies flicker like flying flowers among the bushes and gorgeous birds, like winged jewels, dart from the boughs." But between Fanny and Pierce now lay a chilling feeling of separation, a barrier of deeply felt emotion that could no longer be expressed.

Pierce had allowed Fanny to conduct a number of religious services for the slaves on Sundays, words of hope and inspiration to comfort them in their present life and prepare them for the next one. Sorrowfully she read to them for the last time, and with the same feeling of regret gave Aleck his last reading lesson. He had been quick to learn the alphabet. With a little undercover help from London, he ought to learn to read fluently. If she had done no other single thing she had at least been able to make literate one of these oppressed people, kept deliberately in ignorance—a single flame shining in the darkness. But who would ever come among them again to give them any comfort—physical or spiritual?

On one of her last days, she happened to notice Abraham, the cook, going by with the innards of a particular kind of native fish, of which even the good parts Fanny had thought disgusting to eat. What was Abraham going to do with these horrible insides? Fanny wanted to know.

"Oh we colored people eat it, Missis," he explained.

"Why do you say we colored people?"

"Because, Missis, white people won't touch what we too glad of."

"That's because you are poor and don't often have meat to eat," declared Fanny, "not because you're colored, Abraham; rich white folk will not touch what poor white folk are too glad of; it has nothing in the world to do with color; and if there were white people here worse off than you, they would be glad to eat what perhaps you would not touch."

It was Fanny's ringing affirmation of the Negro as an equal, at a time in American history when so many declared that he was not. With her own eyes she had seen the Negro in his most degraded condition—pathetic, laughable, animal-like in his ignorance. And yet she honored him. Despite the state into which he had been forced, Fanny saw that he was a man with a spirit, a brain, a heart like all other men.

On April 18, 1840, the Butler family started the long journey to the North. Now in Fanny's trunk lay the series of letters to Elizabeth Sedgwick, a truthful, unflinchingly accurate record of life as it was lived among the slaves on a "decent, humanely managed" Georgia plantation.

CHAPTER 22

Fanny's Sacrifice

"MY DAYS ROLL ON in a sort of dreamy, monotonous succession, with an imperceptible motion, like the ceaseless creeping of the glaciers. I teach Sally to read. I order my household. . . . I copy out for Elizabeth Sedgwick the journal I kept on the plantation. I ride every day and play the piano just enough not to forget my notes. Once a week I go to town to execute commissions, or return visits, and on Sundays I go to church; and so my life slides away from me."

Fanny had resumed her existence at Butler Place. Outwardly her existence was calm enough; but the emotional stresses of her marriage with Pierce Butler grew more and more intense. Loving each other as they did, each still had the power to hurt the other.

His presence in a room or the sound of his voice still stirred her heart. The fall of his footsteps could make her start up, eager—or sometimes fearful—at the thought of seeing him.

So it was with Pierce. He had loved Fanny's fascinating eyes, her glorious speaking voice. He had loved her irresistible sense of humor and flashing mind that made her one of the most unusual women of her age. But it was those very mental qualities, her perceptive way of cutting through to what she considered to be the truth, that would not allow her conscience to gloss over important issues such as the question of slavery. The summer after she came back from Georgia Fanny was asked to contribute to a pamphlet to be distributed at an antislavery fair. Fanny complied and Pierce naturally was enraged. What must his family, his friends, the plantation owners who were his neighbors in the South think of this treacherous wife of a slave owner actually publishing her views against the practice?

In the heat of the summer Pierce went to Warm Springs, Virginia, to take a cure for his rheumatism, while Fanny traveled north with the girls to stay again with her dear friends, the Sedgwicks, at Lenox. Just before she arrived Elizabeth Sedgwick received a letter from Pierce, tormented over the state of his marriage. If only Elizabeth could make Fanny see how her strong will, her insistence on holding free and independent views of her own, her continuing to do things that—as she claimed—"answered her conscience" were wrecking their life together. He had, he said, out of his great love for her over the years indulged her far more than any average man would have dreamed of. Now he begged Elizabeth Sedgwick to make it clear to Fanny that she must, *must* submit her will to his—for the sake of their happiness and that of her children.

Elizabeth Sedgwick answered the letter sympathetically and, when Fanny arrived, spoke to her gently and tactfully of Pierce's unhappiness, though she omitted some of the details of Fanny's behavior that had caused him the most pain. Other members of the Sedgwick family also reasoned with Fanny in a friendly way. But a few words from kind friends could scarcely be expected to change the character of one such as Fanny. No one had ever been able to break her stubborn, willful spirit as a child. How could a little well-meant advice turn her into the submissive, tactful wife, living only to please her husband, that Pierce wanted her to be? He had known what she was like when he had pursued and married her. How could he think that she could suddenly pretend not to have a mind of her own, and become a poor, *slavish* creature without character, echoing her husband's views and always agreeing that he was right?

During the summer the Sedgwicks read Fanny's journal of her residence on a slave plantation with grim absorption. Never, it seemed to them, was there a more pressing need for such a book to be published. Brilliantly written, absolutely authentic, it might well swing thousands of wavering minds over to the side of abolitionism. Fanny's book, if published, could be an important factor in doing away with slavery.

But, reasoned Fanny, if her husband had raged over her publishing a simple antislavery essay, what would he not do if this inflammatory journal appeared in print? Moreover she had gone to the plantation, so it seemed to her, as a kind of guest of her husband and her husband's brother. Would it not be taking advantage of them to publish violent criticisms and condemnations of the way they treated their slaves and the manner in which they blinded themselves for reasons of personal profit to the cruelty and injustice of the slave system? In the back of her mind always lay the thought that under the law she had no legal rights to her children. If Pierce Butler wanted to take them from her claiming that she was an unfit mother, or indeed for no reason at all, he could do so and she could not prevent him. Fanny continued to edit and rewrite portions of the hastily jotted down journal, but she took no step toward publishing it.

In the fall Fanny returned to Philadelphia to stay at her brother-in-law's where she had endured the first trying months of her marriage. Butler Place was shut up and they planned to leave again soon for the Georgia estates. Time dragged by and Pierce, who always found difficulty in getting from one place to the next, did not move. Each week Fanny expected to be told to get ready to leave and finally in February on one day's notice learned that Pierce was not going to take her to the South after all. His brother objected to her disturbing presence on the slave plantations; she stirred up unrest and unhappiness. The overseer too thought that she was a danger to "the peculiar institution."

So Fanny returned to her lonely existence at Butler Place, while Pierce made the difficult journey through storms and floods back to the South with his brother. There he fell ill and, with no one to look after him the way Fanny would have if she'd been there, he wrote to her in misery. At the same time she also received a letter from Elizabeth Sedgwick, giving more details of Fanny's behavior that Pierce had said had given him such pain. Once as a girl of eighteen, Fanny had written to her friend Harriet St. Leger, "I think I should be unhappy and the cause of unhappiness in others if I were to marry." Now the truth of her prediction rushed over her in an agony. "Pierce, Elizabeth has written me some of the contents of that letter of yours to her and I felt while reading it as if the iron was indeed entering my soul," she wrote to him at once. "Forgive me, my dearest, dearest Pierce, if I have so bitterly cursed your existence," she begged, not able to see the page for the tears of self-reproach that blinded her eyes.

Spring came on and Fanny was always at her most contented when tending her garden. Pierce returned and the Butlers went to see the great ballerina Fanny Elssler dance a number of performances. The theater had first drawn them together; on these evenings they seemed able to recapture some of that early happiness they had known in each other's company.

The summer passed much as the last one with a visit to the Sedgwicks in Lenox. Again there was mention of her journal. What were Fanny's plans concerning its publication? None, was her reply. Even the Sedgwicks, enthusiastic in the cause of abolition, must see that if she published the journal she destroyed her marriage.

For some time Pierce and Fanny had been considering another trip to England. Charles Kemble was growing old; Fanny could not bear the idea that she might receive the news of his death as she had her mother's—on a piece of paper, three thousand miles away from him. As usual Pierce dawdled, unable to make up his mind to go abroad and claiming that he really ought to return to the South. If he did that, leaving her alone behind, Fanny asked why she should not go to England in his absence. Then news came that Charles Kemble was traveling in Italy with Adelaide, who was singing at opera houses in Naples and Palermo. With the same comic delight in the ridiculous that Fanny possessed, Adelaide had written of rehearsing with "a little, fusty" fellow prima donna who brought with her "a thin shivering dog" that howled throughout their duets together. The prima donna proudly told Adelaide that it had *five* puppies, all of which it had nursed itself, "as if," wrote Adelaide, "Italian dogs were in the habit of hiring out wet nurses." It all sounded great fun to Fanny, who had never been to Italy and longed to see that most romantic of countries, but Pierce, ever conventional, said that it would not be suitable for Fanny to travel from England across the continent by herself and so would not let her go.

As Pierce continued to dawdle, fate suddenly made up his mind for him. Fanny received word that her father had been brought back to London dangerously ill. At once she made arrangements to take one of the new fast steamships to Liverpool in the hope of reaching her father in time. It would not be suitable, a shrewd aunt of Pierce's pointed out slightly sarcastically, for him to let his wife go to her father's deathbed without the support of her husband. So Pierce went too.

After fifteen suspenseful days crossing the Atlantic, Fanny arrived to find that her father was still miraculously alive, but in so critical a condition that the three doctors attending him would not let her go into his bedroom, lest the shock of his seeing her be too great. Incredibly, Charles Kemble rallied, and when a few days later Fanny was allowed to see his old, fond face, she scarcely recognized it. Her father looked like a ghost.

Once the crisis was past the Butler family settled down to a winter amid brilliant London society. They rented a house in the fashionable Mayfair section of London, just off its main avenue, Piccadilly. In strange contrast to her life at Butler Place—even stranger to her existence in Georgia surrounded by filthy, wretched slaves—Fanny was caught up in a whirl of parties, balls, opera-going and visits to fine country houses. Intellectuals, noted political figures, aristocrats all showered the Butlers with invitations. Having friends among the nobility especially pleased snobbish Pierce, and when through their mutual friend the Duke of Rutland, Queen Victoria asked to have Fanny presented to her, it was Pierce who insisted that she buy a new dress (of white satin with red ribbons in her black hair) and hire a handsome display of diamonds "every single stone of which darted a sharp point of nervous anxiety into my brain and bosom the whole time I wore them," as she reported to Harriet.

Such occasions made Fanny terribly nervous. "In great uncertainty of mind I did not look at my sovereign lady. I kissed a soft white hand which I believe was hers; I saw a pair of very handsome legs in very fine silk stockings, which I am convinced were not hers, but am inclined to attribute to Prince Albert; and this is all I perceived of the whole royal family of England for I made a sweeping curtsy . . . and came away with no impression but that of a crowded mass of full-dressed confusion. . . ."

Pierce, through the U.S. ambassador, also arranged to have himself presented on a later occasion, which shocked Anne, the

Butler nursemaid, who thought it demeaning for a free-born American to stoop and kiss the hand of a monarch.

In May, 1841, Adelaide returned home from a series of triumphs in the great opera houses of Italy including the most famous of all, La Scala in Milan. She was the first Englishwoman to appear as a star there and the audience was so enthusiastic that one night when the king and queen were present instead of waiting for their majesties to commence the applause as was the custom, an ovation broke out for Adelaide without the usual royal signal. The reunion between the two remarkable Kemble sisters was a joyful one, and Fanny reported to Harriet of Adelaide, "She is singing most beautifully and the passionate words of love, longing, grief and joy burst through the utterance of musical sound and light up her whole countenance with a perfect blaze of emotion. . . . She has grown very large, I think almost as large as I remember my mother; she looks very well and very handsome, and has acquired something completely foreign in her tone and manner, and even accent."

That summer the Butler family together with Adelaide, her friend the music critic Henry Chorley, and the strikingly handsome and gifted Hungarian pianist and composer Franz Liszt toured through Belgium and onto the lovely lands bordering the Rhine River in Germany. Adelaide appeared as guest star in various opera houses along their route and gave recitals with the dynamic Liszt. Fanny, Americanized now, did not think the Rhine as beautiful as the Hudson River, nor did she see in her travels "anything much more picturesque than the prettiest parts of the American Berkshires."

Adelaide's debut at Covent Garden had been announced for the autumn—another young female Kemble, unknown to English audiences, about to come out in the theater that had always been associated with the great acting family. Her first appearance would be as Norma, a tremendously difficult part in the opera of the same name by Bellini. Fanny was frankly worried. "I cannot help wishing that she would leave the singing part of the business and take to acting not set to music. I think the singing cramps her acting. . . . I suppose my nervousness about Covent Garden is unnecessary," she added with characteristic truthfulness about herself. When asked at this time if she had any desire to return to the stage herself, as though she might be envious of Adelaide's career, Fanny's reply was a resounding, *Never.* "My very nature seems to me dramatic. I cannot speak without gesticulating and making faces any more than an Italian can; I am fond moreover of the excitement of *acting,* impersonating interesting characters in interesting situations, giving vivid expression to vivid emotion . . . and *uttering the poetry of Shakespeare.* But the stage is not only this, but much more that is not this; and that much more is . . . positively odious to me, and always was."

About this time came a worrying and conflicting letter from the United States. The famous abolitionist leader Mrs. Lydia Maria Child, having learned of the existence of Mrs. Butler's extraordinary journal, asked for permission to publish it. Eloquently she pleaded the cause of abolishing slavery in America, something that Fanny's record of life on a slave plantation might greatly further. It was a vital moment in the history of the country and Fanny could give great service to her adopted land.

Fanny hesitated, though the choice was clear enough. Pierce would never forgive her if she allowed the journal to be published. Their marriage would burst apart and under the law he could remove her children from her until they were twenty-one years old.

Taking up her pen, Fanny wrote to Mrs. Child that due to the circumstances of her marriage to a slave owner, one whose management of his plantation was described in such detail in her journal, she could not permit its publication. She offered two small opening chapters, one describing her journey to the South, the other giving her own personal views on slavery.

Thinking he would be pleased, she told Pierce of her decision. But he was not. What right had she, his wife, to openly state her abolitionist views through an abolitionist organization? What would his plantation neighbors think—they, who looked upon the abolitionists as a pack of irresponsible rabble rousers? He wrote another letter to Elizabeth Sedgwick asking her to persuade Fanny not to air her views in public on the troubling question. Opposed to slavery as she was, Mrs. Sedgwick put the loyalty of wife to husband before all else and advised Fanny not to publish even the first two chapters.

Fanny obeyed. Nothing of her journal nor her opinions on slavery appeared at all.

But in this last interchange between Pierce and Fanny something seemed to break between them. They could no longer fight the fact that the question of slavery, which had divided their marriage like an implacable wall of stone from the very first, admitted no compromise. Their love for one another had been deep and passionate, but that love had been tragically destroyed, through no fault of their own, by the great moral issue of the day. Their union, like that of America itself, was dissolved by the question of slavery.

Since neither could change the other the break between them must come. It was only a question of how and when and in what manner it would be accomplished.

CHAPTER 23

A Woman on Her Own

FANNY'S WORRIES over Adelaide Kemble's London debut indeed proved unnecessary. In the autumn of 1841 Adelaide made a triumphant first appearance at Covent Garden and once again a young, dramatically gifted Kemble was the talk of London. Just as with Fanny, whenever she appeared the house was sold out, and so great was her success that Charles Kemble, his health completely restored, became tempted once again by the idea of managing the theater with which his family has so long been associated. Rashly he bought out the interest of the present manager of the theater—"that fatal millstone"—which had exerted a fascination over him like a drug for his whole life. Night after night Fanny sat in the Kemble box hearing her wonderfully talented sister in a variety of operatic roles. Of these performances her Norma, a priestess who has taken a lover and borne him two children, only to be deserted by him for another woman, was considered to be the most remarkable. Often as Adelaide sang and acted the tears would rush into Fanny's eyes. Did she weep not only for the beauty of Adelaide's performance, but out of sympathy for Norma's plight as well? Now, not only had Fanny come to realize that Pierce Butler, the father of her two children, no longer loved her, but he was being faithless with other women as well.

Again her first reaction had been to run away. She went to Liverpool with the idea of taking a ship to America, for, curiously, even with all her family and friends around her, Fanny did not want to stay in London. She thought the life they were leading frivolous and extravagant, particularly as Pierce was now in debt. London brought out the worst in him: his indolence, his irresponsibility, a shallowness to his character that others had seen when she had married him but that she had not. To pay for the elaborate wardrobe she needed to lead such a crowded social life, having used up the none-too-generous allowance Pierce gave her, Fanny felt justified in writing a number of magazine articles and making a translation of a French play. This act of independence, as usual, incensed Pierce, and harshly he reminded her that any money she earned in fact by law belonged to him.

"In thinking over the position of women with regard to their right to their own earnings, I confess to something like wrathful indignation," she fumed to Harriet. "It is true that by our marriage bargain, they [men] feed, clothe and house us, and are answerable for our debts . . . and so, I suppose, have a right to pay themselves as best they can out of all we are or all we can do. . . . I wish women could be dealt with, not mercifully, nor compassionately, not affectionately, but *justly;* it would be so much better—for men."

To the hotel in Liverpool where she had fled after she had discovered his affair with another woman, Pierce soon followed and demanded that she come back, reminding her of the scandal she would create in deserting him and her children. Fanny cared little about scandal, but separation from her children was another matter. She returned with Pierce to London, urging him in turn to make plans for returning to America where he might lead a sensible life that had some purpose. But Pierce, as usual, could not get himself from one place to another, nor could Fanny, with absolutely no say in the matter, make him go.

Despite her great success, Adelaide had already begun to dream of retiring from the stage when she had earned enough money to provide her with a small income and allow her to live in Italy. Instead, that spring she became engaged to a young man of good family named Edward Sartoris, whom one of Fanny's more strong-minded friends thought somewhat lacking in character. Now that her father was once again managing Covent Garden, Adelaide agreed to sing one more season there before making her farewell and venturing onto the sea of matrimony. Ironically, her older sister who had found a career on the stage so odious, feared for the younger one's plan to leave it. What if Adelaide's marriage were a failure, as Fanny knew all too well that marriages could be? "I was surprised to find how terrible it was to me to see my sister, that woman most dear to me, deliberately leave a path where the sure harvest of her labor is independent fortune . . . for a life where, if she does not find happiness, what will atone her for all that she will have left?" Tears streamed down Fanny's face again when Adelaide sang the role of Norma. "If she is only happy after all," Fanny whispered to herself. "But oh, that if!"

The summer wore away in the usual round of visits to country houses. That fall as Adelaide began her final season at Covent Garden, Pierce abruptly gave Fanny the news that he had taken passage for America. When she had everything packed and was ready to leave he announced with equal abruptness that they were not going and moved the family to a hotel. The nursemaid, Anne, was sent back to the United States and in her place Mr. Butler put a governess, Miss Hall, whose pretentious, forward manner Fanny did not like. This woman would now give the girls their lessons, Pierce informed Fanny, who had always greatly enjoyed teaching them herself.

Though the Butlers continued to go out in society, London—ever a city for talk—had begun to gossip about the matrimonial difficulties of the interesting and still young couple. One intimate in Fanny's circle of friends was clever, worldly Charles Greville, who having access to the Court besides a multitude of acquaintances kept a diary filled with slightly sour comments on the great and famous of the day.

"I have been seeing lately a great deal of Mrs. Butler," he wrote, "whose history is a melancholy one, a domestic tragedy without any tragical events. She went to America ten years ago in the high tide of her popularity and when she was making a fortune. There Pierce Butler fell in love with her and she fell in love with him. She gave up her earnings (six thousand pounds) to her father, left the stage and settled in America. And now after wasting the best years of her life in something very like solitude near Philadelphia, with two children whom she is passionately fond of, what is her situation? She has discovered that she has married a weak, dawdling, ignorant, violent-tempered man, who is utterly unsuited to her, and she to him, and she is aware that she has outlived his liking, as he has outlived her esteem and respect. With all her prodigious talents, her fine feelings, noble sentiments and lively imagination, she has no tact, no judgment, no discretion. She has acted like a fool and he is now become a brute; the consequence is she is supremely and hopelessly wretched. She sees her husband brutal and unkind to her, ruining himself and his children, by his lazy, stupid management of his affairs, and she lives in perpetual terror lest their alienation should at last mount to such a height that their living together may become impossible, and that then she shall be separated from her children for whom alone she desires to exist. Among the most prominent cause of their disunion is her violent and undisguised detestation of slavery while he is a great slave proprietor. She has evinced the feeling (laudable enough in itself) without a particle of discretion, and it has given him deep offense."

Poor Fanny. It was a harsh summing up of her situation. Though she never read Greville's lines she probably would have been the first to admit bitterly how true they were. "Brutal, violent-tempered," Greville describes Pierce Butler. Fanny might certainly have denied that this was the kind of man she had married. But had the years of owning of slaves, of living in hypocrisy, of closing his eyes to injustice and human suffering, transformed

Pierce Butler into the brute that Fanny now found herself married to?

For violent and brutish he was, and once more Fanny fled from him to Adelaide, who was living in a house near the hotel where the Butlers had been staying. She sent back an imploring, piteous letter to the man she still loved and who had such power to hurt her: "For God's sake, and for your children's sake, and for your own sake, Pierce, my husband, oh still my most tenderly beloved, let us be wise before it is too late. Show me where I have sinned in this our terrible condition, and mercifully help me to amend it. . . . Let us be friends, let us be Christians, let us return to our duties and to the paths where peace and happiness are found. I implore you by that love which you once had for me, by that unalterable love which I still bear you, and which makes me dread the cause of wrong in you more than any conceivable thing, put away from your heart all evil thoughts and feelings toward me; forgive me and deal with me with righteous and merciful dealing, and spare yourself the reproaches of your conscience and the upbraidings of your better nature."

Pierce's reply was the usual one—she must submit herself to his will and control her own. And Fanny's reply was equally characteristic: "I consider it my duty *not* to submit my conduct to the government of any other human being." And so the bones of the tragedy were laid starkly bare.

Somehow, with the help of Adelaide and Charles Kemble there was a reconciliation. Pierce hired another London house and the season, replete with glittering gatherings of various kinds, went its way. One of its most notable events was the farewell of Adelaide Kemble from the stage—she of whom the great composer Rossini once said: "To sing as she does three things are needed: this" (touching his forehead), "this" (touching his throat), "and this" (laying his hand on his heart); "she had them all." In her retirement England lost one of her greatest operatic singers.

In the spring of 1843 the dilatory Pierce finally announced that they were returning to America, not to Butler Place, however, where Fanny might have found contentment riding horseback around the country and tending her garden, but to a drab, uncomfortable boardinghouse in Philadelphia. It would be cheaper, he said, and Butler Place could be rented to help pay his debts, for which, thought Fanny grimly, he had only his own extravagances to blame. Whether there was any truth in what he told her Fanny no longer knew. His manner toward her had become distant and harsh; and all his actions seemed designed to make her feel hurt and unwanted.

"Anyone would suppose I was in great spirits," she wrote Harriet as she prepared for the voyage home, "for I fly about, singing at the top of my voice, and only stop now and then to pump up a sigh as big as the house, and clear my eyes of the tears that are blinding me. Occasionally too, a feeling of my last moments here, and my leave-taking of my father and my sister shoots suddenly through my mind, and turns me dead sick."

As a fashionable young couple with a large circle of friends, the Butlers gave a farewell party for two hundred guests, with six policemen to guard the guests as they came and went, particularly the ladies covered with glittering jewels. Miss Hall, the governess, who was coming to America with the Butlers, appeared at the party in a black satin dress, Fanny noted, her hair dressed in a number of affected looking ringlets.

On May 4 they embarked from Liverpool to America. Once there, Fanny had hoped that by taking up her old, quiet, routine existence she could still salvage the one wonderful asset in her marriage—life with her children. But in his own country, with his own family and friends to side with him, Pierce began a slow, merciless campaign to take them from her and force her out. Now Fanny was no longer to have a say over what the girls ate, nor how they dressed, nor what books they read. Her mother's duties were entirely assigned to Miss Hall. There were terrible scenes in front of the children and finally when life under the same roof with Pierce became unbearable, and even dangerous, Fanny moved to another boardinghouse. This gave Pierce an even crueler control over her. He limited the times that she was allowed to see her daughters, finally reducing them to one hour. Fanny consulted a lawyer who said that Pierce was entirely within his rights. His only obligation was to give her support, which he did, but in meager fashion. One day he sold her horse, a fine noble animal named Forester, to a livery stable, saying that he could not afford for her to keep one. Again Fanny asserted her fatal spirit of independence: she made a collection of various poems she had written over the years and sold it to a publisher. With this money she bought back Forester, thereby angering Pierce that much more. One day Fanny met her own children in the street. They passed her by in silence. Their father had forbidden them to speak to her except in the one hour of the day that she was allowed with them.

In the summer of 1845 Fanny went away to recover her strength and stayed with her sympathetic friends the Sedgwicks in Lenox. Returning to Philadelphia, she begged a friend to intercede with Mr. Butler asking him to allow her to come back to give a mother's love and proper care to her little girls. Mr. Butler answered her request with an even harsher set of regulations to which she must give her written agreement. Fanny could come back but she would have no say in the children's bringing up; not the simplest kind of order could she give them. In addition she could communicate with him only in writing; he did not wish to hear her voice raised against him ever again. She was also not to see, nor even write to, any member of the Sedgwick family, whom he knew to be his enemies.

Broken, humiliated, Fanny signed the incredible agreement and took up her situation in the family under these intolerable conditions. "He now spared no pains to convince her that in her absence she had naturally lost much of her children's love," writes one of Fanny's two biographers, Dorothie Bobbé. "When a thoroughly bewildered Sally refused to obey her, and Sally's mother protested, he peremptorily ordered the latter to cease her attempts to ruin the child's existence as she had ruined his. When gossip began to grow, trickling through even to Europe concerning his possible amours, he accused her (by letter) of spreading it, and forced her to swear (by letter) that she had not. There was ceaseless strife, growing greater as time went on."

By October, 1845, Fanny had steeled herself to face the truth: not the awful effect of such an existence on herself and Pierce, but what it was doing to the children. For them to see her humiliated every day and spoken to as an unwanted stranger by their harsh father, for them to live in an atmosphere of such hatred, sorrow, and tragedy would ruin their lives. There was only one thing to be done and only Fanny could do it. She must remove the very presence that brought forth such loathing from Pierce Butler and take her sorrowing self away. Even though she might not expect to see her daughters again until they were twenty-one —Sally was then ten, and little Fanny eight—this must she do for them. If their father would not allow her to be a mother to them then the greatest benefit she could bestow on them was her absence.

Somehow she found it in herself to take the necessary action, to put her arms around each of the puzzled, crying girls and say goodbye—for how long? Dazed, she managed to make her way back to her friends in the Berkshires, and such was her unconquerable spirit that despite her totally reduced state of sorrow she managed to give the Sedgwicks pleasure by her company. "Fanny's presence does so improve the quality of life and increase its power by her infinite variety of thought, feeling and expression," Charles Sedgwick wrote to a friend during her visit. "It seems to me an immense good to be with her."

In November her friends took her to Boston and put her on a boat to England. She was thirty-seven years old, without any money of her own, and lacking even a permanent home in her native country. But there was still one thing left to her. However exhausting and distasteful, it would mean that at least she had money—and independence. She would go on the stage again.

CHAPTER 24

The Union Dissolved

> Alone, heartbroken, on a distant shore,
> Thy childless mother sits lamenting o'er
> Flowers, which the spring calls from this foreign earth,
> Thy twins, that crowned the morning of thy birth.
> How is it with thee—lost—lost—precious one
> In thy fresh spring-time growing up alone?

Acacias had been blooming in that May eleven years before when Fanny had borne her first child, Sally. Now seeing the blossoms in Italy where she had gone to stay with her sister, Adelaide Sartoris, Fanny set down these sorrowful lines, as she would others in a similar mood during the terrible first year of her separation from her daughters. Fanny had first gone to England, but her father's constant references to his little granddaughters, whom he greatly missed, and his well-meaning advice as to how to bring about a reconciliation with Pierce were unbearable to Fanny. When Adelaide and her husband urged her to come to stay in their house in Rome, where everything would be new and different to her eyes—where she could live and forget—Fanny went. She had always longed to see Italy and found it as lovely as she had imagined, though strangely full of reminders of America. The spreading Italian ilex trees were like the live oaks in Georgia; a market in Rome reminded her of one in Philadelphia, and when she first saw the vast dome of St. Peter's rising against the sky, she felt the same "tumult of doubt, fear and hope" she remembered experiencing when she had first seen Niagara Falls.

The fact was that she could not forget. She felt herself to be partly American and her daughters, who were still allowed to write to her, were wholly so. That alone was enough to make her nostalgic for her adopted country.

Nonetheless a long visit to a new, fascinating country in company with her adored sister proved to be an effective tonic for her wounded heart and crushed spirits. Never idle with her pen, she kept a journal of her many and varied impressions of Italy, including in the book some of her touching poems that allude to her enforced separation from her daughters. When she returned to England and offered the journal under the name of *A Year of Consolation* to a publisher, much to Fanny's surprise he took it at once. She was always amazed that anyone was interested in her scribblings.

Of her literary ability no less a critic than the great novelist Henry James, who was a friend to Fanny when she was an old woman and he a young man living in London, wrote of her poetry that "much of it has beauty as well as reality, such beauty as to make one ask oneself (and the question recurs in turning the leaves of almost any of her books) whether her aptitude for literary expression had not been well worth her treating it with more regard." *A Year of Consolation* was published in the United States as well and brought Fanny a handsome sum of money. It is a curious book, a landscape, beautifully described in much detail but without people in it. Unlike her earlier journals so filled with vivid characterizations, scarcely a single person comes to life in its pages. The land she walks is empty of human beings; in her unhappiness she preferred to be quit of them.

But to Fanny her most certain source of a good income—Pierce paid her an allowance, but an inadequate one—was the stage, and in February, 1847, she returned to it. Her figure had thickened and time and experience of life had worn down some of her young intensity that had once thrilled audiences. But that same time and experience of life had put in its place a much deeper understanding of the parts she played. Now when she acted the part of Queen Katharine, the cast-off wife of Henry the Eighth in Shakespeare's play, with what feeling she could act her tragic scene in Act Four in which the Queen asks a messenger to give her husband a letter,

> In which I have commended to his goodness
> The model of my chaste love, his young daughter;
> The dews of heaven fall thick in blessings on her!
> Beseeching him to give her virtuous breeding;
> She is young, and of a noble modest nature,
> I hope she will deserve well,—and a little
> To love her for her mother's sake, that lov'd him,
> Heaven knows how dearly.

Fanny Kemble Butler, as she now called herself, made her reappearance in the midland city of Manchester, where she was glad that no one who knew her would be present. Curiously, she felt none of her usual stage fright, only apprehension at the fearful roar of applause that would greet her on her entrance: noise was what her frayed nerves could no longer stand.

Fanny was always her own most astute critic. Of that first return to the stage she wrote coolly to Harriet: "My physical power of voice and delivery is not diminished, which is good for tragedy; my self-possession is increased which ought to be good for comedy; and I do trust I may succeed, at least sufficiently to be able, by going from one place to another, to make what will enable me to live independently, though probably upon very small means."

And so once more she took up the strenuous life of an actress with its never-ending travel, its succession of rehearsals in damp theaters with strange actors, its nightly dose of tension, excitement, and the thought of the morrow when it would all have to be repeated. "I got up this morning with a dreadful cough and sore throat and the effects of overexertion and exposure," she wrote to a friend, "went to rehearsal after breakfast, rehearsed Lady Macbeth and Juliana in *The Honeymoon* (a *dancing* part!); have written to three managers from whom I have received 'proposals'; have despatched accounts of myself to my father and sundry of my friends; have corrected forty pages of proof of my Italian journal; have prepared all my dresses for tomorrow; have received sundry visits (among others that of a doctor, whom I was obliged to send for), and have wished that I had not so much to do."

Bath, Bristol, Birmingham, Liverpool, Dublin—it was all an old story for her. Once during her early acting days these places had been fresh and new to her young eyes and filled with breathless interest. Now she was an experienced trouper working, as she frankly told her friends, simply to make money. As everywhere she acted she made a great success, courageously, entirely by herself, she thus achieved her purpose.

The following year Fanny was asked by the most famous actor in England, William Macready, to be his leading lady in *Macbeth, Othello,* and *Henry the Eighth.* Macready was a violent whirlwind of a performer and Fanny feared for her life in the final scene of *Othello* when the Moor smothers Desdemona. Fortunately Macready turned out to be more considerate than she had expected though she still did not find him pleasant to act with. "He growls and prowls and roams and foams about the stage in every direction, like a tiger in his cage, so that I never know what side of me he means to be," she reported amusingly to Harriet, "and keeps up a perpetual snarling and grumbling like the aforesaid tiger, so that I never feel quite sure that *he has done* and that it is my turn to speak"—a description that suggests how ludicrous modern audiences might have found the acting styles of Fanny's day.

In the spring of 1848 revolutions beset Europe, monarchs were on the run, and there were even riots in staid, prospering England. Fanny, however, was busy with a new and most welcome project. After his retirement from the stage her father had taken to giving readings of Shakespeare's plays cut to a length of about two hours in which he played all the parts. Readings were a most popular form of entertainment in that time, and they appealed to Fanny much more than acting on the stage since she was dependent on no one but herself. As long as her father had been giving them she did not wish to compete with him. Now he felt too old to appear in public any longer and made over his carefully abridged versions of the plays to Fanny. With her reverence for Shakespeare she wished she could give complete versions of the plays spread over three nights, but realized that it was impractical and would not draw audiences.

On March 18 of that year, wearing a red satin dress and seated at a table with a pair of lamps on either side of her script, Fanny gave her first reading at Highgate on the outskirts of London. Her flawless diction, her tremendous dramatic sense, her celebrated voice able to differentiate the various characters, held audiences spellbound. By some uncanny power she seemed to be able to make the people in the plays appear before the eyes of her audiences.

With the vogue for readings at its height Fanny was now assured of a secure living made more easily than by acting; no rehearsals, no need for costumes and makeup, no bothersome fellow actors. Above all she was serving the greatest genius in literary history; nothing commonplace, second-rate, downright trashy marred her dramatic life. Though it annoyed her managers, she insisted upon one condition to her performances: she must read her selection of twenty-four Shakespearean plays in rotation. That way she would not become stale. When the managers wailed that *Macbeth* or *Hamlet* or *Romeo and Juliet* were much more popular than *King John* or *Measure for Measure,* Fanny stood firm.

Having no other expenses than the hiring of an auditorium, Fanny began to make good and steady money which she carefully put away. She also began to dream of returning to America in the hope of making some new arrangement with Pierce over the girls. Surely the passing of time must have softened his heart toward her. He must see that his daughters needed their mother and that it was wrong to deprive them of her. With six hundred pounds worth of engagements scheduled for the spring of 1848, Fanny was planning to return to the United States in the middle of the coming summer when unexpectedly she was served with a legal document. It came from Philadelphia and declared that Frances Anne Kemble Butler was being sued for divorce by her husband, Pierce Butler, on the grounds of desertion.

Fanny was outraged: first Pierce had made it impossible for her to live under the same roof with him and now he was divorcing her, claiming that she had deserted him. She was nothing if not a fighter, and in the heat of her anger canceled all her valuable engagements and once more took ship from Liverpool to contest the divorce.

When the case came up early in 1849 it was instantly seized upon by all the newspapers and blown up into one of the great scandals of the time. Everyone took sides. Had Mrs. Butler, the famous Fanny Kemble, failed in her duties as a wife? Was Mr. Butler a cruel and vengeful man? Resentful and unforgiving he certainly had become. He had drawn up a long list of grievances dating back to the early days of their marriage when Fanny had refused to accept his editing of her first journal for publication. In Georgia, he said, she had openly criticized his treatment of the slaves. In Philadelphia she had disobeyed him by riding alone on horseback along the waterfront, a place not suitable for a lady. In London she had complained of his behavior to friends. Throughout their marriage she had constantly interfered with the raising of *his* children, by giving advice about their food and clothing and had even criticized him for hiring an eminently suitable English governess to educate them. On and on unrolled the document which seemed to some to be the product of a deranged mind.

Nowhere, naturally, did it mention any of his infidelities, nor speak of the duel he had fought over his intimacy with another man's wife, nor his relationship with Miss Hall, the governess, who was also undoubtedly his mistress. When Fanny drew up a similar document in her defense, she made no specific reference to these details of Mr. Butler's behavior as a husband, except to say that early in their marriage she had discovered he was unfaithful to her. Her only plea was that he had deprived her of her rights as a mother and mentioned instance after instance of his deliberately cruel and unreasonable behavior toward her, and of how he had finally forced her out of what was rightfully her own home and away from her children.

Her lawyer gave an impassioned and brilliantly argued speech to the court asking that Fanny's defense be admitted as evidence. The judge refused, though the newspapers naturally seized upon Fanny's plea, thereby swinging public opinion over to her side. Due however to Fanny's defense of the court action, the case dragged on and before there was a decision from the judge the lawyers agreed to a compromise. Fanny, knowing how extravagant Pierce was, had become worried that he would squander all the property that one day should rightly come to his daughters. If he agreed to put part of his property in trust for them and give the income from the trust to her as an allowance, she would withdraw her defense. She also demanded one month—August, 1849—with her girls at a house she had just bought in Lenox near the Sedgwick family. Pierce Butler agreed.

That month was the happiest Fanny had known in years. When it was over she could not expect to see Sally again until May, 1856, and little Fanny in 1858. She was not only no longer a wife—Mrs. Fanny Kemble, she now called herself—but to all intents and purposes not a mother either.

Fortunately, though she had always cursed her profession, she was still an actress. Already during the long period of the divorce, she had begun her Shakespeare readings in the United States. They created a sensation wherever she went. "Mrs. Butler continues her readings to the delight and wonder of her crowded audience," Fanny Longfellow, the charming wife of the distinguished poet, wrote to a friend. Mrs. Longfellow thought Fanny's *King Lear* "a more astonishing proof of her power and pathos than any." But the *Macbeth* was also "very grand and ample, especially the second witch scene, where the 'hell broth' seemed boiling before your very eyes, she gave it with such motion in her voice."

The Longfellows went repeatedly to her performances—*The Tempest, King John* ("too tragic a play for those who have any sorrows of their own," thought Mrs. Longfellow, who knew the tragedy that had beset Fanny's life), and *The Merchant of Venice* at which the sensitive wife of the poet sat directly beneath Fanny and "thought her face was never so beautiful as in Portia's speeches. When it hardens to Shylock it becomes so altered it is like a different mask slipped on." After this performance the Longfellows asked Fanny to supper in their lovely house in Cambridge, during which Mrs. Longfellow gave Fanny a bouquet and Henry Longfellow presented a sonnet he had composed entitled *Sonnet on Mrs. Kemble's Readings from Shakespeare*. It began:

Oh, precious evenings! all too swiftly sped!

Fanny, ever emotional, ever touched by an act of true kindness, was overcome with tears.

From 1849 to 1856 Fanny was a wanderer, a wanderer with a purpose, however, since a large part of that time was given over to traveling about giving her readings in America and in England, Scotland, and Ireland. As a result she was able to turn herself into a reasonably wealthy woman. In the periods when she was not acting she toured around Italy with her sister Adelaide, saw for the first time in the company of Harriet St. Leger the Swiss Alps where her mother had been born, or stayed with friends in Scotland. She was like the Wanderer in the famous poem by Goethe who hears a spirit say:

Da, wo du bist nicht—da, ist Glück.
(There, where you are not—there, is happiness.)

Wherever she went she longed to be somewhere else. If she gazed at "men swimming like magical silver images" in the blue waters of the Grotto at Capri, she wished for the pools of brown-black water to be found in Scottish streams. If she walked through the heather on the lovely highlands of Scotland she longed for the woods and valleys of the Berkshire Hills. She had always been a true romantic—searching for happiness that she knew must always elude her.

But her life was infinitely varied and interesting chiefly because she had long known how to make it so. Her sister's house in Rome was a meeting place for the great writers and artists of the age. Frequent guests were the two poets Robert Browning and his fragile wife, Elizabeth Barrett Browning. Mrs. Browning thought that Fanny in the spring of 1854 was still looking magnificent with her black hair and radiant smile. " A very noble creature indeed," she wrote of her to a friend. "Somewhat unelastic, unpliant to the age, attached to the old modes of thought and convention—but noble in qualities and defects. . . . She thinks me credulous and full of dreams," which was characteristic of the slightly embittered actress not only to think but to say to the poetess.

That year Fanny came back from Rome to nurse her father during his last illness—her father whom she had loved so tenderly and for whose sake she had come to America, with what extraordinary results to her life. A short time later her younger brother Henry died. It seemed unbelievable to her to lose a member of the family younger than she was. Miss St. Leger also became ill but at least Fanny could be there to nurse her beloved "Hal," as she called her, back to health.

As time passed one unshakable fear gnawed at Fanny, who had been cut off for so long from any influence over her daughters. Would they still want to see her? Or had Pierce Butler, as he had already tried to do, been able to turn them against her permanently?

In 1856 Fanny once again took ship across the Atlantic and returned to her little house she called "The Perch" at Lenox, Massachusetts. It was spring. Acacias had been blooming when her first child, Sally, had been born. And now when that girl, blonde and handsome, came to her mother's house in Lenox twenty-one years later the lilacs had put out their lovely, fragrant blossoms.

CHAPTER 25

A Time of Contentment

"OUR DAILY TALK is of fights and flights, weapons and wounds," Fanny wrote to a friend in England from her house at Lenox. "The Stars and Stripes flaunt their gay colors from every farm roof among these peaceful hills, and give a sort of gala effect to the quiet New England villages, embowered in maple and elm trees, that would be pretty and pleasing but for the grievous suggestions they make of bitter civil war. . . . The state of the country is very sad," she added, "but of the ultimate success of the North I have not a shadow of a doubt."

It was August, 1861, four months after North and South, divided like Pierce and Fanny by the wracking question of slavery, had gone to war. Five years had passed since Fanny's joyful reunion with her older daughter, Sally, who had subsequently married a Philadelphia physician named Owen Wister. In 1860 she had presented Fanny with her first grandchild, Owen Wister, Jr., who would one day write one of America's most famous novels, *The Virginian.* In 1858 Fanny had reclaimed her other daughter, who took after her in many ways besides her name. Little Fanny was short, dark, very independent and willful. It was something of a shock for her mother to discover that having been brought up entirely under her father's influence little Fanny remained loyal to his views on slavery.

And what of Pierce Butler? Ironically, while Fanny had become a wealthy woman through her readings, Pierce, always a speculator and gambler, had been wiped out in the depression of 1857. Two years later to pay his debts he had been forced to sell his slaves. That happened to be the same year that the country was arguing the merits of a book called *Black Diamonds,* a series of "truthful and tolerant" sketches of life in the South among the slaves, by Edward A. Pollard, a native of Virginia. He was proud that "the American institution of slavery does not depress the African, but elevates him in the scale of social and religious being. It does not drag him down from the condition of free citizenship and membership in organized society to slavery; but it elevates him from the condition of a nomad, a brute, to that of a civilized and comfortable creature, and gives to him the precious treasure of a saving religion." Mr. Pollard's entire book was in this vein with warm, believable characterizations of slaves of his acquaintance and descriptions of their happy, sunny lives. Mr. Pollard's solution for the rapidly increasing decline of the Southern economy was to reopen the slave trade. That way all the poor whites who could not afford to hold slaves would be able to do so.

All this, even in the year 1859, many people read and believed, as they might also have believed his statement: "The separation of families at the [auction] block has come to be of very unfrequent occurrence." Yet these words were being read about the same time that 421 of Pierce Butler's slaves were herded to the race course at Savannah, Georgia, to be put on the block, their teeth, their muscles and all parts of their bodies examined like so many animals, and sold at auction. A newspaper reporter from the *New York Tribune* managed to get into the sale carefully disguised (Northern papers like the *Tribune* were not even allowed through Southern post offices) and wrote an account of it. True, families were mainly kept together, husbands and wives, that is, but not parents of married children, nor brothers and sisters—and of course not unmarried couples in love. Reading the story in the newspaper Fanny was horrified to see listed one "Sikey"—or Psyche—"aged forty-three, rice hand, sold for 520 dollars." But no mention of Joe, Psyche's husband, nor her two children. In this way Fanny learned that the dreaded separation of the devoted little family that she had struggled so to prevent had in fact taken place. "The inhuman horrors of the slave auction exist only in the imagination," wrote Mr. Pollard complacently and convincingly. When would a true, accurate, detailed picture of the lot of the slave ever be offered to the public?

In June, 1862, Fanny returned with her younger daughter to England, where she found most of her circle of friends, who were aristocrats or members of upper-class English society, mainly sympathetic to the Southern side in the American Civil War. Southerners, they argued, were aristocrats too, defending their way of life, and though no true Englishman could condone the regrettable Southern practice of slavery, still, as everyone knew, it was carried out in the most humane and just way. Among members of the government there was considerable agitation for England to at least recognize the seceded Southern states as the separate nation that President Lincoln and the North were fighting to prove they were not. Some even thought that England should enter the war on the Southern side. So far the British had maintained a neutrality that prevented valuable Southern cotton from reaching the huge mills at Liverpool and Manchester and vitally needed English arms and ammunition from going to Southern ports. But how long would England stay neutral with so much agitation against Abraham Lincoln and his determination to maintain the Union?

In the summer of 1862 when the war was going particularly badly for the North, the London *Times* crowed jubilantly, "The North has tried the great experiment of coercion, and failed; the South has tried the great experiment of independence, and made good its position." Fanny was appalled by the whole climate of her country's thinking, even more so when Lincoln announced in September 1862 that he intended to free all the slaves in the Union in the coming year, and the *Times* thundered: "As an act of policy, it is, if possible, more contemptible than it is wicked. . . . The most consummate folly ever perpetrated by a ruler."

Some time after this the idea of publishing her *Journal of a Residence on a Georgian Plantation* began to grow in Fanny's mind—though not without misgivings. After all Pierce Butler, the father of her daughters, was still alive in America. He had been arrested at the outbreak of the war and jailed for a time on suspicion of having obtained arms and ammunition for the South, but had been released and allowed to resume his normal life provided he did not attempt to go south. Fanny's portrait of her former husband in the journal was scarcely flattering. What would her girls think if it appeared in print, particularly little Fanny, who still felt great loyalty to her father? In addition there were young Fanny's views on slavery itself, altogether different from those expressed in her mother's journal. Was Fanny risking the loss of her daughter once again?

But as usual the demands of her conscience motivated her above everything else. If Fanny could help the British see why Lincoln's Emancipation Proclamation was right and necessary, if she could show that it was untrue that slaves were mainly well treated in the South, if she could do anything to bring over English sympathies to the North and reduce any possibility of England coming into the war on the Southern side, then it was her *duty* to publish the journal. At long last it appeared in Great Britain in May, 1863, and the United States two months later.

Much has been written of the effect that Fanny's extraordinary journal had on the outcome of the American Civil War. A legend has grown up that it influenced English opinion so strongly the South entirely lost the support that it had hoped and worked to obtain from England. Fanny, in fact, is credited with saving the Union by keeping England from allying with the South, and to this day in the South among the people who continue to fight the Civil War and regret that the Union was saved, Fanny Kemble along with other figures such as Abraham Lincoln is regarded as something of a villain.

The real truth seems to be, however, that England's sympathies were swinging to the North anyway, particularly when Lincoln proclaimed the slaves free on January 1, 1863. This released a whole tide of sentiment among the English working class, who from their own position of being downtrodden and oppressed had always despised the idea of slavery. Fanny's book also showed the evils of the aristocratic system, under which only men of property were allowed to vote and who then could enact laws to further their own gain. It is interesting that four years after the publication of Fanny's journal the voting laws of England were changed to allow a great many more Englishmen rightful access to the ballot box.

However much or little Fanny's journal changed the fortunes of the Civil War is still being argued today. Except for a few Southerners who have claimed that Fanny was totally prejudiced against slavery, no one has ever doubted the truth and accuracy of her observations. "The first ample, lucid, faithful, detailed account from the actual headquarters of a slave plantation in this country, of the workings of the system," declared a critic in the *Atlantic Monthly,* when the journal was first published. Not quite a century later when it was republished, the editor of the new edition, John A. Scott, in a brilliant, scholarly introduction wrote, "Fanny Kemble fought, in a difficult time, her own battle on behalf of the brotherhood of man. The journal is a contribution to the antislavery literature which constitutes an important part of the cultural and moral heritage of the American people."

The rest of Fanny's story is quickly told, even though she lived on thirty years after the publication of her journal, not giving up her vibrant hold on life until 1893 when she was eighty-four years old.

These thirty years were mainly a time of contentment for her. She continued her readings on both sides of the Atlantic, though inevitably these became fewer, until she eventually retired from public appearances altogether. She also published a play and a volume of verse, and edited into the form of memoirs all the letters she had written to Harriet St. Leger over the years. These volumes, *Records of a Girlhood* and *Records of a Later Life* are among the richest, most interesting and fascinating autobiographies in English literature.

Fanny's chief preoccupation, however, was with her family. It is true that the question of slavery, just as it had with her husband, lay between Fanny and her younger daughter. She could not approve of little Fanny going south with her father when the war was over to try to "coax" former slaves to work under the new, puzzling system of hiring themselves out for money. Nor did Fanny like it any better when after Pierce Butler had died of malaria in 1867 (characteristically, from not being able to get himself away from Butler Island when the warm weather came on) that young Fanny decided to try to run single-handedly the estates she had inherited, one white woman among a multitude of blacks. But her daughter insisted, just as Fanny, under different circumstances, might have insisted, upon a not altogether advisable course of action. Like her mother, young Fanny recorded her peculiar postwar experience of trying to educate former slaves to hired hands in her book *Ten Years on a Georgian Plantation Since the War*. Somehow their differing views on slavery—perhaps because mother and daughter were so much alike—never seriously intruded on their relationship. Eventually young Fanny married an English clergyman of good family, Canon James Leigh, and though for a time he actually helped her with her Southern experiment, they were eventually forced to give it up and return to England.

To Fanny her daughters with their various children were "magnets" that drew her everywhere they went, except of course when young Fanny went south. At one strange point in her life Fanny found herself moving back into Butler Place, the only permanent home she had ever known since her marriage and where her children had been born. Young Fanny had inherited it and fixing it over with all of her mother's characteristic energy had made it attractive and comfortable. There too were some of the results of Fanny's landscaping zeal of many years before: the long row of saplings that she had planted, now grown into a grand alley of stately trees.

Eventually, however, Fanny returned to England, residing in London and going from there to visit her sister in Italy or making trips to the Alps which she adored, first climbing them, then, when she was too old for that, riding up them, and then, when she was too old for that, having herself carried over their breathtaking heights.

As happens to those who live to a fine old age, one by one those whom she loved were taken from her—her beloved Harriet St. Leger and, incredibly, her equally beloved sister, much younger than she was. Of people who met her in the later part of her life she would sometimes say: "No wonder they were surprised and bewildered, poor things—they supposed I was dead." By then, in the late Victorian 1880s, it was extraordinary to think that here was a woman who had heard Sarah Siddons, her very own aunt, read Shakespeare, who had been drawn by Sir Thomas Lawrence and taken breakfast with Sir Walter Scott. In her lifetime England had changed from a rural, aristocratic country to an industrialized, capitalist one. What it was at the beginning of her life bore little resemblance to what it had become in her last years.

As her old friends died away there were some consolations in the new, inevitably younger acquaintances that she made. Chief among these was the youthful but urbane American writer Henry James, who constantly called on her or escorted her to the theater. James came to admire her "fine anxious humanity; the generosity of her sympathies and the grand line and mass of her personality." All that she said and the way that she said it simply fascinated him. After her death, in a deeply felt memoir James declared ringingly, "She was in the ancient sense, indomitably, incorruptibly superb."

It is characteristic of Fanny that as she approached her eightieth birthday she decided to embark on a new adventure. In her mind remained strong memories of the Sedgwick family and certain tales they had told her of people living in the Berkshire Hills, as well as remembrances of the beautiful countryside itself. Fanny decided to incorporate this material into a novel and proceeded to do so. Called *Far Away and Long Ago,* it was published in 1889 four years before her death. Though it might seem to us today slightly old fashioned, the characterizations are nonetheless vivid and the descriptions beautiful. Nor does age betray Fanny's usual forceful way of writing. Henry James, a writer of immense polish and restraint, was not given to using italics for emphasis in his sentences, but even he was moved to write: "Did *any* one ever produce a first fiction at eighty?"

But that was Fanny Kemble.

Recommended Reading

Unfortunately a definitive biography of Fanny Kemble has yet to be written. Many of her letters and writings exist in collections that were never used by her two chief biographers, Dorothie Bobbé (1931) and Margaret Armstrong (1938) when they wrote their watery studies of her life. John A. Scott has written an excellent introduction to the reissue of her *Journal of a Residence on a Georgian Plantation in 1838–1839* (Alfred A. Knopf 1961) but it is all too short. As he wrote then, "Fanny Kemble awaits the biographer."

Meanwhile in second-hand book shops the interested reader, as I have done, may come across her own fascinating memoirs, *Records of a Girlhood* (Henry Holt, 1879), *Records of Later Life* (Henry Holt, 1882) and *Further Records* (Henry Holt, 1891.) The memoir of Fanny Kemble in her old age by Henry James in his *Essays of London* is also very fine.

Index